Hoof-Beaten Trails

BY

HARRIET E. DOUD

PRIVATELY
PRINTED

Printing Statement:

Due to the very old age and scarcity of this book,
many of the pages may be hard to read due to the
blurring of the original text, possible missing pages,
missing text and other issues beyond our control.

Because this is such an important and rare work, we
believe it is best to reproduce this book regardless of
its original condition.

Thank you for your understanding.

Foreword

The author of *Hoof-Beaten Trails* has been
a keen observer of nearly a century of our nation's progress, for she was born in 1841. Her
father—born within five years of George Wash-
ington's death—could touch hands with the
early settlers who followed the trail of the ox-
team into the new Northwest Territory.

These catch-glimpses of pioneer folk, from
the pen of one who is, herself, but a generation
removed from frontier days, reveal an authentic
picture of a developing community life. The
author says of her book: "Like Topsy, it *'just
growed'* "—gleanings from quaint and amusing
recollections of her girlhood, and from mature
reflections of later years.

This volume is offered as a slender link in the
lengthening chain of memories connecting the
living present with the recent, and with the more
remote, past.

L. N. D.

Contents

PART ONE

CATCH-GLIMPSES OF PIONEER FOLKS

At the Bend of the Trail

DOWN along the century has come the shifting heritage of a broad, rich valley, shaded with forestry and interwoven with brier and bramble and vine. Through the once unmeasured waste of this valley, from a score of coves and streams, culminates and flows the Maumee River, losing itself at last in the far-expanding waters of the Lake. The bark canoe once plied the sluggish stream under the stroke of the Red Man's oar, in sporting and fishing; while the Valley, named in honor of the River, afforded him ample hunting grounds.

From its earliest discovery the Maumee Valley, with its belongings, has borne fruitage by a succession of revelations in nature, art and progress, and many are the interesting footsteps that have beaten a pathway for their followings. Here, from the ruins of an old fort, we may take our observations of this heritage, now fallen in legacies from withered hands that almost touched with finger-tips the borders of the century just past. This marks a battlefield—and these breastworks may have turned the tide of war, to the uplifting of a nation. The surrounding valley presents a study; and just beyond the fort, imbedded in sandstone rocks, are footprints marvelous in form and size, supposed to be impressions from an early geological age though their source remains a matter of conjecture still.

Past Fort Meigs runs the stream which gave name to the shire-town as well as to its vicinity, and "going to the River" came to be taken, by common consent, to have reference to the neighborhood of the old fort, the shire-town, and the Maumee.

In this Valley settled men of later military rank and renown. They raised their cabins, platted towns, and in time opened thoroughfares, constructed highways, and established intercommingling and commerce; while they enshrined their names in titles and charters to be handed down to their children's children, as founders of this, that, or the other town, city, or enterprise.

From these centers proceeded the tribes that peopled a vast section of country, uniting their fame and fortune with others more or less

12

favored than they—often for better though some-times for worse. Out of this evolving medley ap-pear catch-glimpses of ideal characters—manly men, self-poised in conscious obligation, and womanly women who, being found, are worth the seeking. Though famed for deeds of valor, many were poor, and self-support was comely for all. The undeveloped resources of the valley in-spired to energy of life and action, and the fruit of their toil was their satisfying reward.

Out from the prosperous vicinity of Fort Meigs unto the depths of a wilderness, in search of health, wealth, and happiness, went Jacob and Elizabeth Cameron on the morning follow-ing their wedding-day in the Spring of 1826.

Under circumstances less favorable the jour-ney would have been insufferably long, and the bold adventure foreshadowed with dismay. But with all the world centered in themselves, it is not strange that their separation from the crowded hives of their childhood was fraught with pleasure rather than pain. None seemed to their care-free spirits so deserving of sympathy as those who remained at the old-established homes on the banks of the River.

Day after day they journeyed. On—and on—

the oxen pressed the yoke through marsh and woodland and stretches of openings, with here and there a clearing, and now and then the cabins of a few scattered inhabitants. Then, one bright, beautiful day, they turned a hoof-beaten trail and found themselves lassoed into the bend of a winding creek which came to be known in aftertime as the Portage River. Here they stopped to refresh themselves with food and to quaff the sparkling waters. The tender grass spread out before them in tufts of velvet green; bushes and trees seemed bursting into bloom as they beheld. It was high noon and the sun's brilliant rays streamed over a wild retreat where insects swarmed in clouds, and the trill of the toad was answered by the croaking of the frog. Turtles and snakes crawled leisurely from perches on which they were sunning themselves and tumbled into the water with a splash, and fishes played beneath its surface.

The buck, startled at their approach, sprang from their presence, while the doe and her fawn in the distance stood slaking their thirst, knee deep in the running brook. Squirrels clambered over the fallen timbers and scampered up trees where birds in endless profusion held carnival among the branches.

AT THE BEND OF THE TRAIL

To the youthful wayfarers the air was laden with the breath of welcome. By the use of Jacob's unfailing gun, game was captured without delay, a fire was kindled, and in a short time Elizabeth fêted her lord with a feast for a king, while the oxen fed with marked satisfaction on the native grass and drank from the cooling stream.

Wherever they looked the scene was picturesque, and the low hum of the rippling waters appealed to them invitingly. Mussel-shells and periwinkles resembled those of the Maumee River into which, doubtless, these waters emptied somewhere beyond the fort. Distance seemed annihilated as they were cradled into the home-feeling under new settings, and the desire to take possession of their discovery permanently, intensified its realization.

"Let us toss pennies for a spot to pitch our tent and abide here," Elizabeth suggested, and it was done.

"Let us plant a tree that shall grow up with our fortunes and commemorate our adventures when we are gone," said Jacob.

He placed a foot upon his shining spade and threw his whole weight upon it, sinking it down deep into the fertile soil. Turning aside the turf, he produced an acorn which he had carried all in due time the cabin was completed, a half section blazed, clearings made, crops planted, and life in earnest was begun. The "hands" who assisted in Jacob's house-raising were treated with all those marks of courtesy that characterized the older civilization from which he had come, and it followed that rumors went abroad of a goodly spot where dwelt the most well-bred, polite young couple ever married in the Maumee Valley.

In time, Jacob and Elizabeth, as the result of their noble virtues, manifested in good conduct toward others, were surrounded by a community of genteel, well-to-do neighbors with whom to mingle in all the social intercourse of after years.

It is not to be supposed that none but congenial spirits were attracted by the high social order of the new Settlement. There came, not only those who were advanced in accomplishments, but those who were leeches upon the community as well, and settlers with all shades of temper between the two extremes. Among them were the eccentric, seemingly constructed of alternating strata of wisdom and folly. Some were possessed of brilliant, winsome parts, reacting in vain philosophies which were sure to sink them in the end, with all that their zeal had drawn into its currency. Rich and poor, high and low, continued to come, and by the time the acorn was shooting up into a promising scion, Jacob and Elizabeth Cameron found themselves deep in the practical workings of their memorial vows, with an outlying mission fully defined.

Townships were platted and organized, roads were located, districts apportioned, school-houses built. Children were gathered into schools, and the currents of activity and thought became fully established as having sprung from these newly-made settlements in their own rights, and not as the fruits of others. In this consciousness consisted much of the joy with which the early sacrifices were rewarded. It defined responsibility and dignified that which had seemed only an accident of place. It came to be understood and believed that Cameron Settlement had been planted as the result of an unmistakable design of Providence, with a view to a definite end.

The Wizard of the Valley, and the Karls

WINDING along a crooked little stream leading into the Portage River, might have been found a narrow trail beaten by a single pair of broad and clumsy boots. Here and there were footprints of night-marauding beasts, large and small. Now and then, in some unwary nook, the victim of a great iron-jawed trap lay cold and stiff, so suddenly had its death-hinges sprung upon him.

Following back a few paces from the rill was the hut of a lonely wizard. It was built of logs, after the manner of building cabins, but the logs were short. It had a fireplace which was broad in proportion to the house. It had a door and a window, but these were low and close to one another. A bunk and a few rude utensils for cooking and eating comprised its furnishings. Plainly, Martin Terry, the owner, was not situated to make suppers and return invitations, though he was not in the least disposed to decline

19

these from others; neither was he too independent to suggest them, if, in the press of duties, he should seem to have been overlooked. Having contrived a way to a gathering, or "bee," Martin's contribution to the enjoyment of the occasion consisted in an attempt to furnish the most exciting story; and it was indeed strange how a life so narrow could have been freighted with such a wealth of adventure.

For his field of usefulness Martin fell upon the divining-rod, locating wells in a region where he could not go amiss; and he made himself a welcome guest throughout the neighborhood by repeated assurances that underneath the soil lay treasures of silver and gold.

In personal appearance, Martin Terry bore a tall figure and stood erect. His hair was gray and parted in the middle. His mouth was sunken, his chin sharp and protruding, his nose pointed, his eyes small and intense. His manner of speech was to grind through his measured sentences by detached sections, connecting them with a sub-vocal phrase which might have been originally the perversion of an oath, but if so, it had become so dilute as to relieve it of the slightest insinuation of profanity, serving only as an exhaust for the surplus breath left over after finishing his

20

sentences. When animated in conversation, Martin usually became unmindful of himself, clapped his hands upon his knees, with arms akimbo, his body inclined forward and his jaw set for the occasion. In this attitude he wove himself backward and forward, delivering his sentences on the way down, and connecting them on the way up with his home-spun phrase, to which he seemed possessed of the exclusive shop-right.

Martin knew little of books but he had that which served in place of them. He was a practical expert in the geology and zoölogy of the surrounding country—the hero of many a battle with wild beasts, and the prophet who sang to the settlers of wealth and fame.

Separated as he was from the social and civil affairs of the community, and in the absence of common interests or family ties, he was, and remained, a distinct feature of the Settlement, whose peculiarities could be adequately expressed in no other term than simply—"Martin Terry." No introduction could enhance his recognition. Wherever he went, whatever he did or said, betrayed him. It could not be assumed that Martin lived in vain, though he formed only the annex of a community that could well have survived without him. Having the freedom of the neighborhood, Martin Terry was at liberty to pull the latch-string of any house in the vicinity at any time which suited his convenience; and he was possessed of quite as good a faculty for divining meal-times as for locating veins of water, or nuggets of gold; albeit his unbidden presence at festive occasions could well have been dispensed with by over-burdened hostesses.

Among the old-time sociabilities the habit of meeting together for evening visits was a feature of society. It was not the custom for men to go out with their wives in daytime, to dine. After the family supper, however, evening gatherings were quite in vogue, and it is an open secret that those who indulged in recreations at all were no more given to retiring at Christian hours than in modern days. The warning against late hours and midnight feasts probably never will cease to menace the young as a perpetual legacy from one generation to another, being handed down by those who have grown wise through experience or unsympathetic with age.

These visiting parties were a real educational force. Books were few and papers seldom seen. But with all outdoors for an immense zoölogical garden, with lakes and rivers, and all that belongs to land and water and sky woven into their traditions and experiences, who could have failed to profit by the opportunity for discussion which the neighborhood coming-together afforded?

A wedding was especially an occasion for merry-making—a social event of community interest, whatever the rank of the contracting couple. George and Katie Karl, who had been the hired help of Jacob and Elizabeth Cameron, were married at their late employers' house. The Cameron family had given them a plain but appropriate wedding, characterized by all the pretty refinements which it was the custom to bestow upon more pretentious persons, and had set the newly-weds up in housekeeping with sundry supplies. Among these was a variety of second-hand utensils, all neatly scoured and cleaned and set in order in such a way as to seem even more precious for having been used by her who was the recognized queen among housewives.

As George and Katie were settling in their own home, in accordance with tradition they planned a "housewarming." To this they invited such men and their wives as were accustomed to neighboring with the Camerons—knowing few others. Elizabeth was placed in charge of affairs as a guarantee of success, and with right good cheer did the bidden guests take possession of the premises, giving the happy bride and groom a rousing send-off and setting them "on their feet."

A dozen or more men and their wives responded to the summons, and that which sets forth the preliminary preparation of one family will vary little for all. The family of 'Squire Pray, who recently had been raised to that high honor as a mark of appreciation by an admiring public, may serve as an example. When the family supper was over and all the chores had been done, the older Pray boys shouldered their axes, whistled for the dogs, lighted a torch, and were soon off on the trail of a wild beast. The hired man rolled in a fresh back-log and started for the cornfield with his husking-peg in hand, prepared to finish his day's work. The dishes were gathered and washed by the daughters, hash was chopped for breakfast, the floor was swept, and water for morning brought from the spring. Then the long-handled skillet was taken from its nail in the jamb and given to the smaller children in lieu of a popper. The older girls set themselves about the mending and darning by the flickering light of a lard lamp or a tallow dip, such as were coming into use among the well-to-do families of the neighborhood.

Few children were so unappreciative as not to be moved upon by inducements of an approaching party; and not infrequently were their own privileges regulated by their art of conquest, either through winsome persuasion or through persistence in overcoming opposition by force. In aftertimes children were mentioned as being too little to *take,* but in those days, they were spoken of as too little to *leave*—the status being that small children, from "babes in arms" to those who could walk a mile and climb fences alone, were regarded as eligible to social gatherings when accompanied by their parents.

If, in the jostle of walking a log or vaulting a fence on the way, baby chanced to waken and find himself in the strong grasp of his father, and if it so happened that baby did not fancy this situation, he was inclined not to be backward in manifesting a preference for the gentle embrace of his mother. And, being somewhat cramped for modes of expression because of his windings, usually he made the most of his voice. Thus it chanced that not infrequently were the approaches of guests announced sufficiently in advance to allow a host to capture a pullet and have

25

it well under a stew before his visitors should arrive.

Following a well-worn path, all arrived in proper season at the Karl place. Down came the bars. A group of eager, waiting children pressed their faces against the window-pane. After a rasping at the scraper till boots and shoes were scrupulously clean, a loud rap at the door preceded a hush. "Come in! Come in!" was the hearty welcome as the latch-string was drawn; and a jubilee of general gladness broke forth, with "How d'you do?"—"How are the folks?"—"Take a seat"—"Take off your things"—and all that effervescent overjoy which characterized oldtime sociability. One after another the neighbors appeared till the house was well filled; and when the babies had been hushed to sleep and laid away—the men being engaged among themselves —the conversation of the women turned upon the prominent feature of the occasion—the supper.

Quite as many points of etiquette were open to violation by the ill-bred in pioneer days as at any period since, and a woman who could not lend a hand gracefully in the preparation of a feast was considered lacking in parts. Every woman had carried with her a workbag containing an apron in order that she might be prepared for duty. Those aprons, of themselves, formed no insignificant topic of conversation. The sewing was inspected with all that critical admiration which is common at county fairs. The calico that would "wash" was considered superior, and it has been demonstrated that of all the colors then in use, orange and indigo blue are about the only ones that have survived the test of time.

The great iron kettle was hung upon the crane with a full row of pots and pans for fowls and vegetables. George punched the back-log, turning it over as he heaped up a shovelful of live coals in reserve for the baker and the coffee. Katie proceeded with her trial feast, aided by the skillful supervision of Elizabeth Cameron; and Elizabeth was not disposed to dismiss her servant and pupil, and to graduate her into independent livings, till she had seen her safely through her opening party.

After many thrusts at "hide-and-coop," "puss-in-the-corner," and "Simon says thumbs up," the watchful children, who had observed Elizabeth fleshing the meat, rushed upon her, begging for a "piece." With her long-handled fork she good-naturedly took from the kettle a quantity of "drumsticks" and yolks of eggs and chicken liver and bits of breast, which the little folks devoured with relish. Afterwards, wearied with the excitement, the children fell asleep here and there on the floor, and were carefully lifted and tucked into the trundle-bed.

"Who'll make the biscuit?" someone asked. The question went around among the women, and well it might, since bread and butter have been considered the test of culinary art in all ages. A woman might scorch the cabbage, boil her onions to pieces, half stir the potatoes, ruin the squash, sodden the meat, or fail to season the pudding or pie, but if her coffee was unsettled and unsavory, her butter strong, and her biscuits heavy and raw, it was a chance if she ever recovered from the unwholesome reputation of not being able to cook for a feast.

"La's a me!" cried Jane Crow, "I ain't afraid to risk my hand at bread in any shape. I've made the biscuits for all the gatherings in our town for years. There's nobody in our town'd think of getting ready for a bee, without Jane Crow. Give me the ingrejents and get the baker piping hot. If I don't turn out a batch of biscuits that'll melt in your mouths, my name ain't Jane Crow! And I ain't learned to cook for the best provider on the River, neither!"

"That she will!" rejoined Mr. Crow, heartily. "Give her half a chance and I'll wager to eat all she spoils!" This he said, conscious that her success would exalt him among men, quite as much as her among women, for to have made a wise choice in marriage went far toward establishing a record for intelligence in the one making such choice.

Katie had been careful to save back from the churning a quantity of rich cream. It was well. Mrs. Crow, rolling her mutton-leg sleeves to the elbow, called loudly for whatsoever "ingrejents" she desired, and while Katie supplied her wants, and as the other women were setting the table and otherwise preparing for the feast, Jane gave her attention to the critical task before her.

She sifted her flour again and again, while a suppressed smile stole over her countenance, conscious, as she was, that many eyes were fixed upon her, as she ruminated upon the honors with which she was about to grace the name of Crow. Carefully poking aside the air-inflated flour, she called for sour cream, which she proceeded to measure and test. Dipping the end of her finger into the cream, she touched it to her tongue, gazing intently at nothing while a wave of sour sensation rolled over her from the crown of her head to the soles of her feet. Next came the salt. Then the saleratus was crushed fine with a knife on the corner of her kneading-board and scraped into a tea-cup. Over this a little boiling water was poured, when all was emptied into the cream; and as a violent foaming ensued the compound was beaten vigorously and poured into the flour and lightly, though rapidly, stirred until a soft dough was obtained. This was rolled out carefully by handfuls, and cut into biscuit as quickly as possible, then placed in the hot "reflector" and baked for twenty minutes or more.

The undertaking was a complete success, the biscuits seeming not to have stopped rising for a single instant from the sifting of the flour to their removal from the baker, ready to serve. Mrs. Crow was not read in books, but had her exploit been performed at a modern school, under the guise of a "chemical experiment," it would have gone far to place the enduring crown of scholarship on the brow of one who seemed only to have wrought in ephemeral dough.

Toward midnight a most bountiful meal was served and partaken of with relish. In those days people ate to gratify their appetites rather than to observe formal rounds with courses; and while it was considered bad form to be found last at table or to gorge upon delicacies, no conventional limit prevented a good liver from being abundantly satisfied, his restrictions being confined to cake and preserves.

As the women were "doing up the work" and preparing the children for their journey home, the men indulged in stories of adventure. Jacob Cameron told how his father once had been pursued by wolves and cornered all night between the forked roots of a tree, being able to hold the beasts at bay only by kindling a fire and keeping it blazing throughout the long night. He vividly described the manner in which the pack thrust themselves upon his father, gnashing their teeth as he swung his ax to and fro to prevent their forcing a way between him and the blaze.

"You can't tell me nothin' about wolves!" Martin Terry interrupted, assuming his characteristic pose. "I've been chased by them critters by day and by night; and I've tried a-trappin' on 'em, and a-shootin' on 'em, and I've been run down by 'em time and again, but at last I've found a dope that'll fetch 'em every time; and I've been a-fleecin' on 'em for bounty money ever since, and I've nearly made a fortune out of a single pound of the stuff!—"

The narrator suddenly stopped, his eyes fixed

in a penetrating gaze as he turned over in his own mind these victories and marveled at their reality. A mistrustful, thoughtful silence fell upon the listeners, then George attempted to speak. He was interrupted by Martin—

"That ain't all there is on't. I found the woods just full on 'em, and there wa'n't no safety to man nor beast. Thinks I to myself 'if there ain't a change in this respec' my name ain't Martin Terry, and I ain't no trapper, neither!' So I took to buildin' little stables about a mile apart till I had *nine* on 'em in a row; then I got my gun and took fifty charges of ammunition with me. Then I filled up the hoofs of my horses with this dope—*asafetida*—and started 'em on a dead run for the nearest stable and I hadn't more'n got there till I heard the wolves a-howlin'. So I rode into the stable and fastened the door and got ready for battle—when, *here they come*! a-tearin' along after the stuff; and I begun a-shootin' at 'em till I killed *three* without movin' out o' my tracks—and the rest took to the woods for their lives! Then I started out under a keen gallop for the *next* stable—and sure enough!—the critters came a-sniffin' and a-rantin' along wo'se than before;—and so I kept on till I'd shot *f-i-f-t-e-e-n* out o' the pack!—and since that time I don't want no better fortune than a pa'sel o' wolves after me—if I've got the *dope* for 'em on hand! *Back-ash!*"

Martin's voice rose with the thrill of the chase, and his final explosive ejaculation roused the trundle-bed. In the general confusion which followed, the party broke up, the guests dispersed, and George and Katie were left alone to carry on as best they might in the new life so auspiciously begun.

The pathway of George and Katie Karl was strewn with unfolding incentives to a higher life. The sturdy, unlettered farmer-mechanic grew more gentle in spirit, more patient, kind, and teachable, as he and Katie patterned their lives after those who had the advantage of superior opportunities. Their conduct and purpose changed, and the sweet, ennobling virtue of gratitude permeated their household, because of the kindly interest of others with whom they came in contact. "Be thankful it's no worse," George was accustomed to say when misfortune overtook him. And not infrequently did he extract questionable satisfaction from the fact that others seemed worse off than himself, as though this inducement were a part of the message.

" 'Squire Pray tells me," George said to Katie, "that it takes at least three generations to build a family, and that each is as but one stick in the timber of a house. It goes this way: Solomon, the son of George, the son of Jason; or it's David, the son of John, the son of Hiram, the son of David the elder. It counts much for families to be welded together, and to progress by making up in one generation what they lacked in another. It's as though a new door has been opened to me, leading into a world where all have an equal chance in the making of a successful life."

Soon the associates of George and Katie were influenced by the latter's aspirations. Many who could not have been reached by those whom they conceived to be their "betters" were moved to nobler living through free-and-easy contact with these social go-betweens. But the Karls had drifted into a chronic pout, because, forsooth, their eldest daughter, upon becoming "hired girl" for the Prays, had not been freely admitted to all the confidences of the household. In provincial phrase, she had not been made "one of the family."

On general principles, to be communicative on suitable occasions, helpful according to one's measure of ability, and respectful and courteous

34

in spirit at all times, should, for ordinary purposes, satisfy a reasonable claim of one person on
another. The more intimate friendships will
naturally be governed by special aptitude, with
which none have the right to interfere. The extent to which one is able to support personal
friendships is circumscribed, growing choicer
as the interest intensifies, until a point is reached
where familiarity on the part of outsiders becomes invasion—a point where individuality is
fortified in natural rights, and self-protection
against the outer world is justified.

This George and Katie did not understand.
They expected a glow of smiles, a share in the
privileges of the family, a full exposé of confidences, and an occasional outburst of affection,
in addition to Gretchen's pay, as a reasonable return for a "hired girl's" service. Anything short
of that seemed ill-treatment on the part of the
employer, deserving of resentment on the part
of the one employed.

Naturally, Gretchen could not be made one
of the 'Squire's family, because she was born one
of another's family. Had it been possible to make
her a member of both, she would have enjoyed a
distinction of privilege which her employers
were powerless to bestow upon even their own

35

children. For outsiders, either servants or guests, to share equally the confidences of the household, is a most fertile source for the demoralization and disintegration of the home life. Home has its inner court, sacred to the family. In exclusiveness consists its sacredness.

When it was observed that the Karl children were reared in tenderness, and encouraged in study; that borrowings were conscientiously repaid; that the family group attended the means of grace regularly, being devout in manner as well as thoughtful in mind; and when it was noticed that the Karls took to reading, and finally to needlework and music, and that their home gave visible proof of tidy housekeeping— when all these evidences of a growing refinement were felt and realized, the Karls were accepted, even among those from whom they thought themselves separated by a social barrier. When they ceased to bolster themselves up by a mock profession of "being as good as others," and made room for gratitude, for which there was ample occasion, they began to build to the best class of the community, for it is always a pleasure to lift up those who are disposed to benefit by an outlay of one's time and strength.

The children of George and Katie grew up in

36

a God-fearing home, accustomed to such advantages as their parents were able to bestow. Solomon, the eldest son, was tall and ungainly—in the language of his associates, "bashful and green." He suggested a weed sprouting out from under a board—his face was of a milky white, his hair was light, his forehead high, his mouth elastic, and his ears adjustable.

Could Solomon have found himself installed at the head of a home of his own, nothing would have been more to his liking. But the conventionalities of "being struck," "going sparking," "popping the question," "getting spliced," and "being belled"—these were too much for his courage. But Providence makes no mistakes, nor owes apology to any man. A new neighbor moved into their vicinity, and George Karl, in accordance with the hospitality in vogue, sent Solomon over with a sparerib roast, as an offering of welcome. A mess of pork, a hunk of venison, or a rabbit stew were customary gifts to newcomers in these parts.

When Solomon in all his glory presented himself at the front door and knocked with a resounding blow, the most beautiful girl he "ever clapped eyes on" answered the summons. At once a sense of contentment with his surroundings

37

pervaded his soul, and that which had hitherto seemed but a mean village, became exalted. A series of borrowings sprang up, which served little purpose other than to multiply visits between the two families, and ere he was aware of it, Solomon found himself the object of attraction to his charming friend Susie. Upon the whole he was glad, though what so divine a creature saw in him to admire, was more than he could tell. Yet he hoped some day to be worthy of so much beauty and elegant ease.

The heart is a strange unfathomable vault, though the most frequented place in all the world. The lovely image that lingered in the unexplored recesses of Solomon's soul fitted awkwardly in its new settings. Every look into the mild, blue eyes ministered rebuke to his clumsy hands, his cowhide boots, his ungainly bearing.

It transpired, most unaccountably, that Susie became exceedingly fond of Solomon's sisters, frequently visiting them on Sundays, which gave him an embarrassing consciousness of being under watchful surveillance. His most ambitious thoughts seemed to stand out in open view, so illy were they concealed. Added to this was the painful apprehension lest some member of the family should display weakness that would react

38

against his prospects—a near-tragedy that almost occurred.

It was on a particularly languorous, late Sabbath afternoon that Solomon inveigled Susie away from his affectionate sisters' oversight and they sauntered toward the lower meadow, beyond which the western sky was fringing the horizon with crimson and gold. Stopping to rest on the long work-bench back of the corn-barn, Solomon dangled his legs awkwardly over the far end of the seat, while Susie sat at a quartering angle beside him. Little Jamie Karl, slipping around the other side of the barn unobserved, sidled along the bench, nonchalantly and listlessly taking in the landscape. It was a moment of critical anxiety to the families of both the young people, who felt that Solomon's devotion was at last to be rewarded. They had waited breathlessly lest some straw of interference should fall on the tide of true love, which was reputed not to run smoothly at best.

Little Jamie hitched closer, as Solomon seemed about to murmur words of endearment; when, suddenly, his father's thundering voice startled him into action. *"Ja-mie! Ja-a-MIE-EE!"* his excited parent frantically boomed. "Don't you *know* better? Go *'way!* Go *'WAY!* and quit your

39

scouring 'round! You *bother* your brother!"—a mild rebuke that may have changed the course of destiny.

The nuptials of Solomon and Susie advanced swiftly. The approaches to the great occasion lost their terrors for Solomon. Even the "belling" stood out in the light of a playful prank, since a basket of apples, topped with a delicious frosted cake, left near the improvised fence across the road, would quiet the most boisterous uprising. It was to be expected that those who were un-invited would deliver their surplus venom in ringing bells, shooting off guns, and blowing horns, to say nothing of that invaluable noise-producing accomplishment, the sawing on tarred and rosined boards.

The wedding took place at the home of the bride. George and Katie, in their turn, provided an elaborate "infare" when the honeymoon was over, as a fitting send-off from the parents of the groom.

Though sometimes the way was dark, George and Katie Karl were headed in the right direc-tion for the fulfillment of their hearts' desires concerning the upbuilding of their family. Un-able to formulate a definite future, they had but

40

to live on and hope on, trusting the guidance that holds all destinies in its hands.

Solomon and his wife removed to a larger city, where his natural abilities and industry were rewarded with increasing responsibilities. By the time George and Katie felt the tuggings at anchor in making for broader seas, they perceived that a rift had come between them and their son. The children of Solomon and Susie wore gloves, and shoes and stockings the whole year through, and they dressed according to the vain pomp and glory of the world! As long as he lived, George Karl himself had never indulged in so needless and extravagant a luxury as boughten "galluses." Throughout the heated season, it was his custom to appear in his shirt sleeves, displaying to advantage his homemade suspenders, which were knit by Katie in two sections, joined at the back by a buckskin plastron, from which they diverged right and left, forming complete hangings for his loose and baggy pantaloons.

Chopping wood outdoors, and knitting indoors had been the symbols of economy throughout the Settlement, with the elder Karls and their friends, and George held tenaciously to these opinions of thrift and comfort. At the time of his

41

son's marriage, George felt that he could endure seeing the young couple succeed or fail, standing on their own merits, living within easy reach for the donating of a jag of wood or a sack of flour. But when their course was shifted, and one after another of the old ways was cast off in favor of the new, the test proved hard to bear.

In after years, when the two families met, there was little in common between them, though this fact was more apparent to the oversensitive older family than to the younger, who, doubtless, in their turn, would cling to antiquated ways, and history would repeat itself. In the end, however, when George and Katie found the strong arms of Solomon Karl about them in their declining years, they forgave Susie her pretty refinements, and at last their light went out in the midst of what, to them, seemed the dawning of an age filled with miracles and wonders.

Lazy Joel, Lying Jack and Mother Arpatia

RANGING back from the hut of Terry the Wizard might have been found the dwelling place of a family trio familiarly known as Lazy Joel, Lying Jack and Mother Arpatia. Whence they came and whither they went, nobody knew and nobody cared. They were mentioned as having been discovered by Terry on one of his divining expeditions and they came to be regarded in the light of a geographical blaze, defining the northern boundary of a civilization which Joel considered was unlikely ever to push beyond them.

The Settlement was fast becoming a popular center, attracting many by its fertility of soil, its natural advantages, numerous clearings, and above all by its high order of social life. Contrary to Joel's expectations there came a time when one clearing fringed upon another, till he and his belongings were swallowed up and projected

43

into a stirring neighborhood—a result that could not have been accomplished by any effort of his own.

At first Joel felt strangely uncomfortable, not to say rebellious, in the midst of the push and progress with which others had taken the liberty to engulf him. When the true situation finally dawned upon him, however, with an air of affected naturalness he made a virtue of necessity, and availed himself of the uplift which had been thrust upon him so unexpectedly. He appeared to regard this field as a most desirable arena in which not only to further his own enjoyment but to benefit others as well.

No sooner did Joel find himself embodied in a community which had begun to develop assemblies and associations looking to the well-being of all, than a sense of self-respect began to tingle through his sluggish soul. He found himself perfectly willing to sacrifice his private interests for the good of the community at large—not so much to broaden his sympathies as to shift them about into more prominent settings.

It was strange how an outlying mission could divert one's interest and energies from his own household till he forgot his contract on behalf of his family. But in this emergency, what were a

44

wife and son compared with a broad, widespreading community in need of his services?

If his beloved Arpatia, whom he must have sworn to love and protect, wished the wood chopped, or the roof mended, or the sweep-pole toggled, Joel was sure to have business of a public nature on hand—a town meeting might go all wrong without his advice; a neighboring logging had no one to oversee its men; a "raising" needed someone to drop an occasional word of encouragement or to "hoist the captain" when it was over.

Surely Arpatia could not stand in the way of the public good, with her small domestic affairs which attracted little or no notice from others, the more especially since Joel was at home nights and mornings—and what more could a wife ask? He had his place at the table and his chair at the fireside, into which he fell by the force of gravitation at suitable times. It counted for victory in self-denial that he so frequently dined at home when his enlarged sphere afforded ample opportunity for a well-rounded meal among his thrifty neighbors. Moreover, he often chose voluntarily to put up with the stinted rations Mother Arpatia was certain to serve him at home.

45

In time, Joel acquired a practical though somewhat limited knowledge of the value of sunshine and out-of-door air. To avail himself of these he preëmpted a seat on the dooryard fence which he cushioned with an undressed pelt folded back upon itself, and on this he frequently sat, whittling and meditating for hours in succession. But he was not limited to his own fence, for there was scarcely a farm in all the Settlement which had not some rail or log or stump or stone ceded to Joel's use whenever he chose to yield to gravitation at that particular spot. Nowhere was he so much at home as when perched upon one of these pedestals, overseeing the work and considering the benefits accruing to others through their fortunate find.

Mother Arpatia was of a tall and graceful figure which would have borne up under a more elaborate wardrobe than that which it was her custom to display. Her brief morning toilet usually lasted throughout the day. Her general wrap was a long, loose cape; and for headdress she affected a slat sunbonnet, equally suitable for all seasons of the year owing to its alternating features of thick and thin. Once to have seen Mother Arpatia branded recollection for life. As a house-

46

wife it is fair to assume that she was a success in proportion to her opportunities. The family's earthly possessions were easily assessed since they had squatted on just so much land as Joel was ambitious to till, and the desire to gain the whole world was not a weakness through which he was exposed to the attacks of the Adversary.

Mother Arpatia meant to be truthful and honest, but she was sometimes overcome with extremities; and while she would not take that which belonged to another to gratify an unlawful propensity, to do so for a *living* fully justified the demands of her conscience. Their overgrown son Jack appeared to be a supplement to his parents, imbibing the virtues of both. He was equally at home overseeing the "hands" in the fields, robbing a nest, or contriving proof necessary to establish the innocence or guilt of one accused, for which service he was open to inducement. So naturally did he take to the kinks of his calling that it was often more than a match for a shrewd pettifogger to locate the missing links in the chain of his testimony.

In a cabin roofed with thatch through which the rain poured and the sun shone, lived this trio when at home, enjoying all they knew of life

47

since contentment proceeds from within. To adapt themselves conveniently to their surroundings constituted the sum of their happiness.

Lazy Joel could not accommodate himself to the spirit of the progressive community and in time he fell out. No one knew where he went but it was assumed that he afterwards adjusted himself to some neighborhood where a man who had plenty of this world's goods for a fortnight ahead, was not expected to exert himself for bread he might not live to eat; and where Mother Arpatia's wardrobe was good for another turn, being new to those who never had seen it; and where Jack's stock of anecdotes might gain fresh currency. One thing was certain—they were in no danger of settling where people were unwilling to accept them as they were.

Possibly their departure was hastened by an unforeseen event calling for undue exertion on their part. A group of lads returning from a midnight chase discovered sparks leaping from Joel's chimney. Running with might and main, dripping with perspiration, they reached the cabin just as the roof was bursting into blaze. The family, all unconscious of danger, was peacefully sleeping to the accompaniment of crackling flames.

48

LAZY JOEL AND MOTHER ARPATIA

Shouting at the top of their voices, the young men finally succeeded in rousing Joel, who, being apprised of his danger, slowly raised his head from his pillow, and, resting upon his crooked elbow, drawled out:

"The pail's at the end of the bench, boys, but you'll have to draw the water with a rope—the sweep is untoggled."

The shock of this accident was not without its fruits. As Mother Arpatia, released from the bondage of household tasks, was clearing away the debris on the following day, she felt her soul kindle with the spirit of progress and thrill with a fine sense of the esthetic. Under this bewitching spell she accepted a challenge from a wandering huckster and traded her offending cook-stove for a charming toy clock.

It was Joel's misfortune to be entirely unlettered though he was not wanting in ingenuity. He had, in the course of his career, invented a system of hieroglyphics which he alone could interpret, and by which he was remembered long after his form and features were forgotten. From his preëmption of the top rail of the fence till the day of his departure, Joel never abandoned that tripod as a situation favorable for sunning himself and for ciphering out his jokes prior to their

49

currency. It was utilized also in keeping accounts of his numerous borrowings.

Borrowing and lending were common specifications under a law of neighborly kindness, and Joel was predisposed to try the spirit and test the forbearance of those with whom he was surrounded, by his habit of continually roaming about for the necessities of life. From a pinch of salt to a bag of flour, he was quite certain to be "just out" no matter when he was met.

Sitting upon the fence, the geography of the Settlement appeared as two hemispheres to the right and left of him. If a neighbor to the right loaned him aught, a notch was cut in the end of the rail pointing to that hemisphere. If the debt was due in the opposite direction, notches were cut in the corresponding end of the rail. Upon making a payment the proper notch was whittled out, and once a year it was his custom to audit his own accounts, strike a balance, and turn over all to profit and loss, when the boards were cleared in a wholesale slaughter of notches and the record begun anew. Only for his timely disappearance, eventually he must have whittled himself into the ditch.

When Joel and all that were dear to him had left the community, his top rail was set up as an

Ebenezer in commemoration of the family, to magnify their tenets into object lessons for others. Their mission having been accomplished, they passed from sight soon after the fire and never were seen or heard from again.

The Reign of the
Van Cotts

ADJOINING the older Settlement, in a favorable bend of the Portage River, there had been surveyed a section for another farm. The felling of timber, the sound of the broad-ax, the swish of the trowel, all told of a thrifty neighbor. In turn the house, the crib, the pens, the stable, the sweep-pole and the well, were finished. Then a long silence marked the abandoned spot till one day in early Spring a mover's wagon hove in sight. It was drawn by oxen and contained all the portable belongings of Gideon and Sally Van Cott, including a portion of their family. A caravan of beasts was herded along by their sons, at the rear. The strangers proved to be the colonists who were about to take possession of the neighboring improvements and there plant a center from which to propagate a school of ideas in accordance with their own notions of life.

In nationality the Van Cotts were Dutch. They had adventurous natures and were given to launching out into unknown seas regardless of consequences. A small farm in a stinted corner of another's blaze never would have satisfied their ambitions. Broad acres, plenty of service, and room according to their strength, were the only considerations that offered any inducements to this markedly independent family.

Arriving at the farm, they made ready at once to occupy the premises, when the reign of the Van Cotts began. Gideon was large and coarse, loud and impulsive, though underneath his rough exterior he was tender, sympathetic and approachable. He was accumulative and thrifty. His tongue was almost constant in the delivery of his messages of thought. Being given to noise and blustering, shouting and singing fell from his lips at random. He took to prayer as one falls upon a romance, and his devotions were to him a pastime most delightful.

Mrs. Sally Van Cott was short, stout, and sturdy of stature. It is supposed that she was resolute in spirit though she was not familiarly known, holding, as she did, a most stoical indifference to the existence of others.

A broad enclosure marked "No trespassing," with a well-guarded gap for Sally Van Cott to pass in and out at her own caprice, was all she desired. She asked no odds of others, nor did she exact tribute from them. Had she misfortunes, she had plenty of courage to bear these, and she had nothing better to recommend to others in like affliction. "An eye for an eye and a tooth for a tooth" was her law of justice, and the shortest cut to the settlement of any question. She believed what her five senses taught her and nothing more. She had no concern for the frivolities of fluctuating fashions. A bonnet was intended to keep off the sun and for nothing else, a hood was for warmth; and whatsoever answered these purposes was good for all ocasions so long as it lasted.

From the time of their settling upon their farm till the day of her death, Sally Van Cott wore her dress with straight, narrow skirt, short waist and mutton-leg sleeves; and on her head a muslin cap with a plain, broad ruffle, devoid of other ornament.

Like Gideon, Sally must have inherited one marked vein of refinement which, in her case, took expression in a passion for flowers. Her gardens bloomed in beauty and the variety of her sets, slips and seeds, was quite incredible in view of the times and her surroundings. She had been known to journey forty miles—much of the way

54

on foot—for a single variety of plant. Yet in all this she had nothing in view but to gratify a natural propensity of Sally Van Cott. Should a neighbor chance to steal an ambush from which to gaze upon this paradise of birds, butterflies and blossoms, it was no fault of Sally's if the dogs were not set upon him at once.

Gideon was fond of circulating among people, and, being naturally intelligent, he kept himself quite abreast of the times. When cook-stoves came into market he was first to purchase one, which Sally accepted without remonstrance; for when she *did* turn over a new leaf, she was sure to set her stakes far in advance, out of sight and hearing of others against whom she was liable, otherwise, to jostle. It was long before any save Sally Van Cott enjoyed the luxury of a cook-stove.

Gideon and Sally each had a religion though neither had a theology. He was like the poor Indian "whose untutored mind sees God in clouds or hears Him in the wind," while Sally contented herself with a religion of material things. Each believed in looking forward to a dying hour. Gideon had hope in his devotions, but Sally's preparation for death consisted in an outfit of shrouds, with tucks and draw-strings made

55

adjustable to the precarious growths of a stocky family. Many a time did the maternal hand, parboiled with "washing day," deal a deafening blow to little ears, followed with the stern injunction to "get out of that chest and quit mussing the shrouds!"

Gideon was ever alert for the supernatural. When awakened from a sound sleep by a bright light shining in at his window, accompanied by a hissing noise, he sprang to his feet, shouting the children awake with the terrifying announcement that Gabriel had come! Falling upon his knees he poured forth his soul in loud and fervent prayer. But Sally, prying into the material cause, discovered the source of alarm and, dealing her suppliant spouse a vigorous shaking, she commanded him to get up at once, and save the meat—the smoke-house was on fire.

Martin Terry had a keen rival in Gideon Van Cott, for hunting and trapping not only served as an escape valve for his surplus energies, but these also yielded him a bountiful revenue. He hunted by day and by night till he became as familiar with the habits of wild beasts as with those of domestic animals. On one occasion he rapped at the door of Jacob Cameron at midnight and, pulling the latch-string, entered unbidden.

"I've treed a coon!" he announced with his characteristic volume of voice. "Lend me your gun, Jacob."

Punching the overhead beams with his cane, and battering the stair door with clenched fist, Gideon shouted:

"Get up, boys! Go with me if you want some fun!"

Half a dozen pairs of feet came down upon the floor above with a single spat. The dancing about gave evidence that the expedition was likely to be well manned. Scampering down the dark and crooked stairway the youngsters landed at the bottom with hair starting in a pinwheel and scattering everywhere, as they hurriedly seized their boots and sorted their mittens by guess.

"Now while I am warming myself, boys," Gideon continued, "you get your Testaments and read a chapter. We'll have a season of prayer before we go. But first put on the tea-kettle."

In vain did the boys expostulate, in view of the danger of losing the beast.

"There's no danger at all," Gideon explained; "I've got him safe up a tree with a fire under it.

57

The dogs are tied to its roots. He'll not come down. Punch up the back-log and turn to the first chapter of John's Epistles, and read it verse about."

There was no retreat, though a midnight prayer service under the auspices of Gideon Van Cott was the last thing to have suggested itself to the lads retiring under the old home roof.

Verse about, the chapter was read, and Gideon proceeded to make a long and devout prayer. He prayed for safety and success to himself and the boys, for benedictions upon the remaining household, and for broader fields of usefulness to all. By that time the kettle was boiling, and he quickly drained his cup of tea. Devotions over, dogs, boys and guns joined in the hunting spree which lasted till morning but which returned the victors laden with spoils.

In spite of lack of opportunity in his early days, Gideon was well up in general information, and unusually versed in the Testament, a book of which he was passionately fond, carrying it about with him wheresoever he went. There was a time when no regular religious services were held in the community, yet occasionally a traveling exhorter took compassion on the settlers and threw himself out of his way on a long journey,

58

to preach them a sermon either at the school-house or in some barn. Gideon, being dissatisfied with so stinted a measure of gospel opportunity, volunteered his services to preach on Sunday as occasion offered. At rare intervals Sally even permitted him to hold a meeting in their own barn, which meeting she sometimes attended, laying aside her sunbonnet and occupying herself with knitting, apparently unconscious of the presence of others, while Gideon preached.

It was Gideon's custom to mount his horse or to send one of the boys from house to house whenever he felt drawn to hold services, scattering news of the meeting appointment for morning or early candlelight as the case might be. However, it is not to be supposed that Christianity became for him an unfailing rule of conduct under his own ministry. "Repentance" was his favorite theme; but it was plain that Gideon needed his own medicine, for never was there a time when a few buckets of sap from his sugar bush were not considered sufficient excuse to forestall an appointment; though, be it said to his credit, he usually notified of his detention by sending word through a cheap "hand," lest the congregation should weary in vain waiting. Finally his appointments came to be conditioned upon the measure to which Providence might visit his camp with sap.

When, in the course of development, churches were organized and ministers appointed, Gideon's addresses took rank accordingly; but it is fair to presume that, with all their misgivings, the community was none the worse for being tided over into established usages by the volunteer ministries of Gideon Van Cott. His was a life content with stirring things up; and whatsoever he conceived in his own brain, or heard of through others, he was quite sure to set going for the uplift of humanity. With his many-sided gifts, each manifest on a limited scale, his name became the synonym for all the trades and professions which developed in after years; albeit men themselves narrowed in proportion as their chosen specialties widened into monopolies; whereas Gideon's gain was that he had himself laid the foundations for them all.

The Christian virtues that develop into sweet forbearance and kindly consideration for others as age creeps on, were wanting in Mrs. Sally Van Cott, and her declining days were comprised in closing out one material interest after another, to the end. She believed that, in dying, she should "surely die"; and the clods of the meadow finally covered her over, under the shadow of that faith.

Gideon, in dropping each earthly ambition as it passed from his reach, replaced and overlapped it with some outlying possession in fruitage of "the promises"; and when at last his days were numbered, his hands were folded to rest and his eyes closed in full faith, believing that, falling upon sleep, he should wake up in the morning.

Jerry Brooks and the

District School

THE school-house had been built in the foreground of a ten-acre field, and behind it meandered a path trending along the banks of the Portage River.

Back from the main road stood the cabin of Jerry Brooks and Molly, his wife. The house was constructed of round logs. It had two doors on opposite sides of the main room, with a window beside each door. A fireplace had been built of field stones; and against the end of the cabin, a lean-to had been thrown up and sodded over in lieu of a cellar. There was a well of never-failing sulphur water, fed from a spring and curbed about. From this well, water was drawn by means of a bucket attached to a rope.

Mr. Jerry Brooks stood six feet in his coarse, clumsy boots. He had a fair skin, blue eyes, hair streaked with gray, and a kindly face usually beaming with a smile. He was favored with a liberal allowance of good nature and forbear-

62

ance, for which he had abundant need in view of the strain to which his equanimity was frequently exposed.

Mrs. Brooks was a beautiful little woman with piercing black eyes, pearly teeth, and jetty ringlets falling upon her neck and shoulders in perfect regularity, not a hair out of place. Always neat and tidy, she was never less than presentable at the door however suddenly she might be surprised by a guest or a passer-by. Naturally delicate, of an exquisitely fine, sensitive, nervous temperament, she was easily disturbed by irregularity and disorder.

The Brookses had no children of their own, yet frequently they made places for dependent relatives, so long as it was agreeable for all concerned to live together. Had they possessed a family in their own right, the strain of trivial annoyances might have been relieved. In place of nights made restless by apprehension of barn doors being battered open by the wind, or shocks of corn flattened to the ground, Mrs. Brooks might have composed herself sweetly to rest under the consciousness that the cap-strings of the baby's bonnet were tied in a well-balanced knot, with the ends thereof exactly of a length; that the sleeves of its snowy nightgown were

63

evenly extended about the little wrists; and that its restless toes were tied together to prevent irregular development of the tender limbs.

The touch of baby hands all their own might have inspired and expanded her soul with an uplift of personal interest. The petty things that absorbed and vexed her out of all proportion to their passing importance might have sunk into the background, in comparison with family interests really worth while.

Lacking these, Mrs. Brooks was left to gratify her mothering instincts upon whatever came within her reach. While not cross and domineering, she was painfully alive to disorder, and her fine sensibilities were stimulated mainly by being exercised upon things inanimate and devoid of resistance. Every piece of furniture seemed to know exactly where it belonged. Mrs. Brooks' table linen and her floor were scrupulously clean at all times, and Jerry was none the worse for finding it a necessity, if not a pleasure, to see that his boots were in keeping with the general decorum of the house, when he came in from the field or the barn.

With all the excellent qualities of Mrs. Brooks, and with all her real affection for Jerry, however, it cannot be denied that his happiness frequently

64

was threatened by the intermittent attacks of nervousness to which his wife was addicted. When Jerry rolled in a crooked back-log unwittingly, Mrs. Brooks found herself unable to sleep until it burned in two, in spite of Jerry's repeated attempts to straighten it, obediently punching and prodding with his long iron poking-stick, in the vain hope that some blazing knot might give way. The log being over-long in the first place, was endless torture—a huge, crooked, green back-log, elevated at an angle of forty-five degrees and skewed against the masonry of the fireplace. And to add to Mrs. Brooks' discomfort, the end of the log sizzled with sap as the heat increased.

It would be ungracious to give Mrs. Brooks no chance to vindicate herself. The real situation was one to excite pity, rather than contempt, for an orderly housewife compelled to live at one end of a footpath, with a district school at the other end, and with nothing but an orchard between. Switches used in professional service were quite as likely to resemble the sprouts from Jerry's orchard as a birch from the neighboring woods, where, during the recess intermission, the art of gashing the rod of correction to mitigate the force of the blow flowered to its fruition.

Mrs. Brooks raised fowls, and while they frequently cackled in the neighborhood of the school-house, never an egg could be found, though shells were plentiful—with egg-eating animals a doubtful explanation. Not until their geese were disabled for flying because the last available quill had been plucked for a pen, were Jerry and Molly at peace. Should a board be desired for a seesaw, some lad was sure to remember that Jerry Brooks had a pile behind the woodshed. If his fences were torn down to accommodate the younger boys, or to expedite the flight of older ones, Jerry had but to put these up again —a matter of small consequence. A quid of Jerry's wheat made an excellent substitute for spruce gum—and Jerry's barn furnished an unending supply. A barbecue in the woods was a great lark—and Jerry, had he not corn for roasting, and turkeys in abundance?

Jerry's belongings came to be mentioned familiarly as "the barn," "the ax," or "the ladder," as if in joint ownership. Equestrianship, then coming into vogue, was well received, both sexes taking kindly to this accomplishment. Jerry's horses, of assorted sizes and ages, ran at large, and were pastured on the Commons. If he wished to ascertain which of his colts were halter-broken,

66

or which of them cantered, or galloped, or balked, he had but to whistle for a boy, and the information sought was forthcoming.

When it became apparent that Jerry's available horses would be inadequate to supply all who desired such exercise, necessity invented the novel expedient of tying strings of bark to the horns of cattle. A coat or a shawl, with a surcingle about the middle, served as saddle. This means of locomotion proved more certain and safer than the catch-chances of horse-power. The cattle quickly learned to guide and trot, and, seeming to enjoy their new vocation, upon the whole made very desirable roadsters. Excitingly satisfactory results could be produced with a pin surreptitiously thrust into the thigh of a placid old "bossy"—especially if its rider was a shy little girl, whose pigtail braids, tied with gay ribbons, flopped wildly out behind.

Even though Jerry's bank-house was robbed of its winter store, and a mus'rat was cornered in the mill-pond, so that the pond went dry when the creature dug through the dam, Jerry kept on friendly terms with his tormentors, assuring Molly that it was "better any day to be spliced out than to be cut off." And Molly's tear-storms shifted their quarters, while he made ready a "rolling-barrel," all smooth and champered down inside, for an accidental drowning.

The youngsters were not long in discovering that their homes were far too distant to permit of returning for singing school, spelling school and evening entertainments in the school building. As a result, helplessness became epidemic; so picnic suppers were improvised, and many a self-invited guest added an embarrassing strain to a hostess sometimes driven to great extremities. The Brookses never refused to lend to these picnickers, thought it must be confessed that the latter were shamefully negligent in returning their borrowings, and Jerry's cows failed in "pailing" simultaneously with the ushering in of the new school year. Accidents were not infrequent, and in the absence of a professional surgeon, many a gash did Jerry bind and many a torn garment did Molly mend, while he administered boneset tea or poulticed bruises with pokeberries. Many a time was his house converted into a hospital for the maimed and mangled whose injuries resulted from depredations upon his own property.

Skating on the river was a favorite winter sport. Though girls had not, in early days, aspired to this art, as did their brothers, they were not debarred from an even more delightful pleasure. A young man felt himself knighted if he could lead forth a pretty girl clinging to one end of a long stick, while he guided her rapidly over the ice, holding fast the other end of the pole.

It was Jerry's custom to cut holes through the ice for the watering of his stock. A light freeze rendered these holes deceptive traps for the unwary. It was an exhibition of no small dexterity, and required no little courage, for an adventurous admirer, after securely tying on his skates with a halter, to dart lightly over the glassy surface of the ice, and, under the momentum gained, skim swiftly across the thinly-glazed water-hole. Nor were his advances always crowned with success. An ignominious plunge into the frigid water often required the assistance of a despised rival to rescue the frantic swain, clinging desperately to the crumbling fringes of the suddenly-opened gap.

That was a fortunate week when no one was disabled by accident, chilled by swimming, poisoned by vines, or strangled in diving.

He whose recreations are confined to the gymnasium, with no beast or bird in flight, and with no hound at his heels, with no ditches to jump, or fences to climb, has little conception of the invigorating zest for books that the oldtime school afforded.

The district school was a success according to the standard of its day. The ferule and the birch, while approved instruments of punishment, were in no case permitted outside their conventional uses. "Standing on the floor," "wearing a dunce-cap," "sitting on nothing," and such like afflictions, were optional with the teacher, but if worse came to worst, there was nothing that quite took the place of the birch.

Never was there a time when a constituency was more sensitive to the failings of a teacher than in the early days of pedagogy. Did a pedagogue fall short in "doing a sum," or in locating a river, or writing an acceptable copy, or mending a quill pen, his influence was lost. Not only must the master be possessed of knowledge and discretion, but he must have, also, the physical unction to command respect and enforce his decrees. He was expected to be well up in social accomplishments, generous and given to hospitality. And if he should be likewise up in music, this was accounted in his favor.

Parents frequently visited the school—sometimes merely to leave the baby to be "minded" by an older sister, assuring an uninterrupted day's outing for themselves, but more often out of consideration for the education of their children. The master was expected to entertain visitors by exhibiting copy-books and comparing the progress of his pupils, dwelling diplomatically and at length upon the marked advancements of the children of his guests. No experienced pedagogue would fail to recognize in this his opportunity to make a lasting friend.

Classes were put on display out of their regular turn, and a parent seldom left without enjoying the privilege of hearing his own children read and spell. It was considered a discourtesy not to invite guests to take part in the teaching —otherwise a teacher risked seeming void of confidence, not only in his school, but in his visitor as well.

Co-education was the rule, but all schoolhouses were divided into a "boys' side" and a "girls' side." To be found misplaced, was quite certain to locate a culprit serving out a penalty, unless he should be found at the end of a bench, under the appearance of necessity, in order to be seated at all. Even then, his innocence was barely admissible, and he was not altogether free from suspicion. Religious congregations, which customarily assembled in school-houses or in barns, observed the same rule, and the man who had the courage to break over this unwritten law and to sit in meeting beside his wife, lived to see his name enrolled among the "beacon lights" of local history.

Noontime and recess were eagerly anticipated intermissions. Then seesaws, though general property, were often a source of contention—the transient ownership being vested in the right of discovery and possession. Sometimes a whole gang of boys ran madly through the woods after their leader, though none could give an intelligent reason for the chase.

If swings should be found occupied, the late-comer had merely to improvise one of his own. He could climb a slender young tree to the top-most branches. If the limb bent under him, well and good. If not, another lad stood ready to follow—and another—and another—till the sapling was sufficiently loaded to weight it down. Then, all hands grasping the branch firmly, with a spring at a signalling yell, they let their united weight fall, in an effort to bend down the tree. Since there was a tendency to overestimate their avoirdupois, it was no uncommon sight to behold a row of squirming lads dangling in midair and shouting lustily for reinforcements, which were usually forthcoming. The whole school would have sat on the limb to bear it down, if necessary, such was the spirit of comradeship. Not all bore the test of faithfulness, however. A counter-attraction frequently relieved the sapling of its burden—all save one inexperienced lad, suddenly left kicking wildly, silhouetted against the sky.

Intuitively the boys and girls worked and played in separate groups. The former might peel bark and construct summer play-houses for their sisters, by twining these strips about trees, or bring baskets of leaves with which to carpet the floors, or build tables and fashion sideboards for furnishings; but the brothers devised for themselves a counter-attraction on the Commons. A missing guide-board from the public highway perchance found a resting place nailed to a tree at the turn of the cow-path. It read:

20 rods to the Hardware Store of
Reed & Cameron
Country Produce exchanged for Goods.

A well-defined "business block," outlined in bark, teemed with activity. The youthful merchants did a rushing business in old iron, cast-off tools, implements, and bits of broken pottery, from a nearby dump.

Shortly after the opening of this school-boy enterprise, as Jacob Cameron was enjoying his daily siesta, tilted back in his hickory chair on the shady side of the porch, Martin Terry approached.

"Good day, Terry." Jacob's greeting was perfunctory, as he motioned his guest to a seat on the steps.

"Well, if the madam wouldn't mind to set on an extra plate for my supper," Martin began, "I'd be pleased to relate a new kind of experience I've stumbled onto within the past few days."

"Exactly so," Jacob encouraged.

"Well, t'other day my dogs struck the track of a rabbit. I followed on till I found myself run into the play-store cobbler shop of the district school on the Commons. Imagine my surprise when I tell you that there sot Gideon Van Cott in his sock feet, and young 'Liza Loper a-sewing fresh ears onto his boots as fast as she could pull out the needle and stick it in! Says I, 'What does all this mean?' *She-she,* a-lookin' up pert and winsome, 'Hain't you never hearn o' Amazons?' Says I, 'Amazons! What be they?' *She-she,* 'You

74

don't appear to be well read up in history.' Then Gideon took out his Testament and spoke up, and says he, 'Here in Acts sixteen-fourteen you'll find that women were in business, and no fuss appeared to be made over it, either, in them days. We seem to be goin' back to old customs.' Says I, 'What's become o' the boys' store of Reed & Cameron?' *She-she,* 'That's all gone into the hands of girls. It just appeared that as soon as we come in at the front door, the boys broke out at the back door. They won't work with us, no-how!' 'What's all that for?' says I. Then Gideon spoke up for it was gettin' around to his line. Says he, 'It ain't chivalry, nohow, for boys to compete with girls. Before they'll do it, they'll clear out.' Says he, 'Girls get their livin's at home and they can afford to work for pin money if they please, but boys have got to get out and be lookin' to the support o' families some day, and they can't stand such competition, nohow.' 'Well, what's their proposal concernin' a livin?' says I. Then 'Liza Loper spoke up, and *she-she,* 'They don't appear to strike anything but to be pesterin' o' Jerry and Molly Brooks.' Then Gideon, says he, 'I s'pose they've got to get rid o' their steam somehow. If they can't make a livin' keepin' store, there don't appear to be much left

75

for 'em to do on these Commons.' Says I, 'I guess I must be goin' or the track'll get cold and the dogs can't follow it. But by the by, can you'ns tell me where to find a market for a fresh rabbit?' Then 'Liza Loper spoke up, and *she-she*, 'Yes, if you'll go to the boys' old hardware stand at the end of the cow-path, you'll see the sign o' Sabina Summerfield. She'll pay the highest price for hides and pelts.' 'Well,' says I, 'things appear to be a-turnin' 'round! Do you call this a reform or a swap?' Then I started on. But before I got out o' sight and sound o' 'Liza Loper's giggle, I met Sabina a-comin' in with a fresh rabbit, half alive and kickin', and she was headin' for the store as tight as she could jump. Says I, 'Hello, Miss! Where'd you get that rabbit?' *She-she*, 'I saw a dog on its track and I just thought I'd cross the Commons and might be I'd catch a beast for market. Don't you sometimes like a rabbit stew? I'll sell it cheap, bein' it's you. If you'll give me a fip-and-a-bit, it's your rabbit.' Says I, 'I reckon it's my rabbit anyway, bein' it's my dog that ketched it, and I was on its track till I stopped in to see 'Liza Loper new-ear Gideon Van Cott's boots.' 'Well!' *she-she*, 'I won't be small with you and I don't want no hard feelin's about it. We'll go snooks. You may finish killin' it, and dress it

76

and take out the in'ards, and you may have the carcass and I'll take the pelt.' And I'll be bound if she didn't turn 'round and take me in pardner and close me out to myself at her own figger, before I'd time to think what I's about! But *back-ash!* I just took that carcass and went over to Jemima Jump, and says I, 'If you wouldn't mind to accept this mess from me, I'd be pleased to come 'round this evenin' and help you get away with a rabbit stew.' *She-she,* 'It's very kind in you, Mr. Terry, I'll do it with pleasure, and thank you besides.' And if you'll believe my word, I broke right down and went to cryin', it put me in mind o' the time *she* used to call me *Mister* Terry, before she went off on missionary work among the Injens!"

"Exactly so," said Jacob.

"That ain't the end on't, neither—not by a long shot. Some time later I's goin' across the Commons and when I come to Jerry's bars, there stood Tom Simkins and Ben Karl and your Job and a pa'sel o' others a-tossin' the broomstick. And I says, 'What's a-goin' on here?' Says they, 'Where's your divinin' rod, Terry? We're consultin' the oracle to find somethin' to do for a livin'—somethin' the girls can't get away from us.' Says I, 'It ain't sellin' rabbits you want,' says

I, 'for t'other day Sabina Summerfield took me in pardner and sold me out to myself at her own figger, right before my face and eyes. And first thing I knew, she'd hired me out to work for myself, and paid me off with the carcass of my own rabbit, and taken the pelt herself, and for the life o' me I can't see through it yet!' By that time the dogs had struck a fresh track, and I was a-feared Sabina'd get me in pardner and specelate on me again, so I says to myself, 'Martin Terry, it's rather risky to pass the time on the Commons'—so I went on, and left 'em workin' it out."

Elizabeth appeared at the door, as a suggestion that supper was ready, but Martin was too absorbed in his theme to heed her gentle presence, and with hands on knees and arms akimbo, he continued weaving himself backward and forward, connecting his sentences with his homespun phrase, as usual, while she waited patiently for the end of his story.

"Well, it's this way. Perhaps I ain't the one to advise, but nevertheless it's my opinion that if the girls ain't a l-e-e-t-l-e careful about swaps, they'll reform their sect off the face of the earth. This is a big country, by all accounts, and if we

78

that drove out the Injens ha'n't no use for 't, now
that we've got it, it's mighty clear that we'll wake
up some mornin' to find ourselves a-crackin' sage
brush for a hidin' place from them that's got the
next best chance to it.

"I tell you, friends, I have strange dreams over
yonder in my hut these days. T'other night I got
to wonderin' where all the dead Injens went to,
before Jemima got among 'em to turn 'em into
angels, an' to teach 'em your kind o' idees about
the hereafter. I went to sleep, an' it appeared to
me plain as day, that I saw a great, open hunting
ground. An' there they all was—Injens, dogs,
game and all—an' they was on the chase just as
they are here; only when the Injens shot into
beasts it 'peared to be as much fun for one as
t'other, and neither of 'em had the kind o' bodies
to suffer with, and shootin' clean through 'em
didn' 'pear to hurt 'em one item—not one item
did it hurt 'em—and they 'peared to put in all
their time just a-caperin' about in that kind o'
style!"

"I really must interrupt you," Elizabeth
broke in. "Your story is very interesting, Martin, but perhaps a warm supper will compensate
for the interruption."

"Sit up! sit up! and have some supper, Terry," Jacob urged hospitably, and he fell upon a service of grace.

The incorporation of a new village school freed Molly and Jerry Brooks of the annoyance of their lively young protégés. Instead of the expected happiness, however, they found themselves aging in the absence of that youth and vigor of which they had been suddenly bereft.

Day after day, in Spring and Autumn, Jerry sat under the guide-board at the forks of the road, or leaned upon the stringers of the bridge over the river, watching another generation of boys and girls on their way to school. But the hours were filled with heartache, for those who had preyed so lavishly upon his time and solicitude were conspicuously wanting. In his tender moods Jerry often said to his tearful wife: "Perhaps it may fall to our lot, Molly, to keep our latch-string out for them in a world where parting is no more."

Though the trundling of railroads and tramways had not reached the vicinity of Jerry Brooks, from every quarter of the globe there came forty trains of thought a day, pitching their cargoes of memories into the heads and hearts of

Jerry and Molly, to be delivered in dreams of the night. Glimpses, bordering on the prophetic, linked the future with the past, and, waking, Jerry saw them realized.

There came a time when Jerry forgot his protégés, and if one asked concerning them, he would stare the questioner in the face, wondering who was meant. Ere long Jerry closed his eyes for the last time on earth, and moved up, where, in his delirium, he had insisted he was going— to a fairer land, to make ready his house for the welcoming of the district school.

It mars the pleasure of recollection to realize the bitter loneliness of Molly's last days, though with her ripening, she lost, somewhat, her sensibilities to earthly pain and joy, and received with gladness her summons to join Jerry in their mansion in the skies.

The Crows in
Prosperity

MR. SAUL CROW and his wife Jane, the famous biscuit maker, possessed, happily, a large family of orderly children, nurtured under an exacting régime—a régime tempered with push and conceit which were employed principally in turning everything to its own account. Children, in the early days of the Black Fork Settlement, were utilized in serving their superiors; thus a family grew up with a sense of mutual dependence and helpfulness. Each Crow child understood perfectly well his part in the performance of adding a quill to the wings of the Crows.

The Crows had an uncanny gift for publicity. Nothing could be done for miles around without the name of Crow attached. The Crows had either seen or heard or done something in connection with it—or the Crows had *not* seen or heard or done something about it. Had a good work been accomplished, the Crows had approved it from the beginning. Did an evil de-

82

velop, the Crows had felt "jubious" all the while concerning the case. Every little Crow understood thoroughly that, whatsoever his appointed task, it was set with a view to his aptness for elevating the family at that particular point, thus adding one more headline to the currency of the Crows. Not only did truth and verity come to cringe at every joint under such pressure, but an outlying mission soon developed, having for its end, however well disguised, however self-deceived, a broader and more widespread propagation of the name and fame of Crow. If Elizabeth Cameron had made a pan of biscuits to melt in one's mouth, her womanly dignity would have prevented boasting; yet if Jane Crow had but passed through the cabin during the process, the efficacy of her shadow would have been heralded to the ends of the earth.

In course of time guide-boards, paid for at public expense, stood beside every cow-path, pointing to a newly laid out allotment—*Crowville*—which, it was fondly hoped, would become the metropolis of a united community. Later, when the points of the compass were discovered to overlap the originally established Settlement, the names of the latter's worthy founders seemed to lose luster under the swoop of the Crows. This

83

concerned the Camerons little, however, so long
as they were conscious of being instruments
through which a kind Providence was pleased to
furnish brain and brawn and fiber and character
to a rapidly developing republic in the heart of
the great American continent. A glory that must
be fanned constantly, Elizabeth thought, is not
worth the ignoble toil it costs, since a few re-
moves, at most, will annihilate all forever.

Jacob and Elizabeth were unmoved by the
shoppy fame of this rising star, though sometimes their eyes were blurred by its brightness
and their ears deafened with the hollow echo of
its name. Strangers who came into their midst
were led to believe that none were so great as
the Crows; though the more conservative inhabitants valued the older friends in proportion
as contrast to their more pretentious neighbors
became marked. The former lived in their hearts
—the latter preferred to live on their tongues.

A climax was reached in the ambitions of the
Crow family when they discovered the magic
power of the Press. Privileges were purchased at
once, that they might the more satisfactorily be
heralded abroad through the columns of the
only newspaper within circulating distance of
the Settlement. Every weekly edition brought to
84

the scattered families of the well-to-do community some news of the prosperity of the Crows, for which all parties cheerfully paid. *The Times* appeared to live in their interests. Saul Crow's cattle were reported to be the best fed in all the county.—The Crows were about to build an additional lean-to.—The Crow girls were expert in "starting the pipe."—The Crow boys excelled in chopping wood.—The Crow baby had been seared by a live coal that fell from its grandmother's pipe.—The Crow horse could climb ladders.—The Crow cat had five toes.—And so on and on, week after week.

In a surprisingly short period, through the far-reaching influence of the printed word, upon which Saul had blundered by accident, the Crows found themselves the center of attraction to a large outlying public. Many a sight-seer did they entertain, who went away to brace up the political candidacy of 'Squire Crow. The title " 'Squire" came as a social honor to him, rather than as a civil function. It was Mrs. Crow's forethought that her husband should be raised to this distinction in a political sense as well, not only for the exalted rank which it would confer, but for the financial return which it would bring, in aid of the family support.

85

No sooner had the 'Squire whetted his appetite for the spoils of office, than he set about to explore the currents, to find a still broader and loftier sweep for his rapidly widening fame. He was persuaded that to represent the State in its chief executive halls is greater by far than to move about in the limited function of a county 'Squire. *The Times,* which had been his indispensable friend and ally, was instructed to espouse his cause and to manipulate its bellows accordingly. An editor would have been considered a novice of his craft, were he not to publish a series of innocent boastings which should have been patent to all, serving only to gratify those of highly inflated imaginations concerning themselves, especially since he was twice paid for it, wherein consists the profit of advertisement. Therefore *The Times* became the obedient servant of the candidate, in breezing him through his perilous undertaking.

Saul had learned that nothing so surely stirs public sentiment and enlivens a campaign, as a social question. It perplexed him, however, to figure out a plan for uplifting the people, not knowing whether they would wish to be lifted that way or not; with the prospect that his party would lose, should he miss the mark. The responsibility was disheartening. There appeared to be no end of work and worry in politics.

Mrs. Crow, as usual, was equal to the emergency. Flinging a bunch of shavings and tufts of hickory bark into the open crater of the fireplace, to add a glow of welcome to the home-coming of her perplexed husband, she suggested, helpfully: "There's the Loflin children—folks are disputing whether they should belong to their father or their mother, now that the parents are parted. You could espouse the cause of the downtrodden mothers."

The 'Squire slapped his knee enthusiastically. "You've struck it, Jane! The Hon. Saul Crow from Crowville will present a bill praying that in case of a family disruption, the children shall belong to the mother. Nothing in the world will draw upon the sympathies of men like the sufferings of women and children. Even men who beat their own wives and starve their own children cry like mourners over the distresses of others. It's all plain sailing now!"

And so it transpired that the next issue of *The Times* headed its political column with the touching lines descriptive of a slave mother's children:

HOOF-BEATEN TRAILS

*They are not hers, although her blood
Runs coursing through their veins.*

With this stirring battle-cry, was the startling announcement that Mr. Saul Crow, familiarly known as the 'Squire, was about to yield to the overwhelming importunities of representative men of the county, and accept the nomination for legislator of the State. A brief statement of his views on social emergencies was included, with his avowed intention to serve the commonwealth to the best of his ability. The announcement ended by assuring the public, which he had been instructed to place under obligations to himself, that Mrs. Crow joined the candidate in extending to them all the hospitality of the Crow home during this campaign.

But the women were aghast at what seemed to them a deliberate plan, supported by law, for the breaking up of their families—offering as a premium to a man inclined to be wicked or slack, that, in forsaking his wife, he should thereby be exempt from the burden and responsibility of the care and support of his children as well. *The Times* reaffirmed its faith in the broad sympathies and sterling worth of the candidate; and announcement was made that Mr. Crow would visit the neighborhoods in the interests of his campaign, according to his convenience and their expressed desires.

Mr. Crow started promptly on his rounds. But, feeling a little "jubious," he observed the precaution to take with him Mrs. Crow also. As the 'Squire and his estimable wife rode from house to house, the very dogs barked angrily at them. They were pointed out as disturbers of the peace and invaders of the security of the homes.

At the entrance to the wide gate and broad avenue leading to the spacious mansion of Gideon Van Cott, they alighted from their buggy and Mr. Crow hitched his horse. Mrs. Crow snapped the dust from her garments and folded her long, green veil back and forth upon itself mechanically, forming a canopy over her bonnet. Leering out over the premises, they prepared to run the gauntlet with cackling, crowing, squawking and gobbling fowls, and howling, barking dogs.

The 'Squire had no sooner raised his hand to lift the knocker, than the door was burst open by the sudden exit of a half-grown lad in rapid flight, hard pressed by Mrs. Sally Van Cott with her steaming paddle, which she had snatched hurriedly from a kettle of boiling suds. Turning her wrath impartially upon the startled guests, she shrieked excitedly:

"Are you the folks around to back up the daddies to turn out their babies to go naked and starve?"

Angrily brandishing her dripping scepter, she set on them a pack of eager hounds, and it was a source of profound thankfulness to the campaigners that they miraculously escaped with their lives.

A caucus was called to discuss the difficulties into which the campaign threatened to plunge the community.

"This is a woman's question," suggested a quiet listener.

Mr. Crow nodded.

"I propose that the wives and mothers be called into consultation."

Mr. Crow nodded emphatically. But when the 'Squire found that the plan would admit Sally Van Cott, as well as Mrs. Jane Crow, he insisted there ought to be a *picking* of women for a time like this.

Jacob Cameron argued that the remedy for troubles of the class under consideration is not

90

in providing contentment under an evil, but in strengthening the bond that holds the family together; that the weakening of this bond, the State, as ultimate guardian of the children, should seek to prevent in the interest of its wards; and any pettifogger who violates a sacred trust, by encouraging the separation and breaking up of a family, for a fee, should himself be amenable to the State.

"You must not lay people's tangles too much to heart, Saul," said Jacob kindly. "We learn the grace of patience through trials and forbearance. Everyone loves women and children. They cannot get a generation away from mutual dependence. But don't worry if the millennium is not set up in our day. You must not let it crush you, if you do not overcome all the sins of the world in a single term."

With the preliminary campaign completed, the election of Saul Crow became an assured fact, since nothing could withstand the combined strength of his blissful domestic relations, the forceful influence of *The Times,* and the loyal support of Jacob Cameron, whose tactful persuasion had steered Saul's enlarging mind into safe and proper channels. All that the Hon. Saul

Crow now needed was judgment to direct his sympathies aright, and firmness to hold him in poise.

A successful election, with its accompanying sudden access of power, brought to the new legislator an expanding compassion and broad-reaching brotherliness that embraced the whole world. The Hon. Saul Crow's cup of joy overflowed in abounding lovingkindness toward his unfortunate fellowmen. It was borne upon him by degrees that the proper course of helpfulness was to reconcile the dissatisfied by giving them some constructive work to do; not that one man should do aught for any other particular person —as though he should first find work for himself, and then add to himself the burden of another who is under equal obligation to find work for himself. It was rather that Saul could now manifest a right spirit in a free-will offering of helpfulness to humanity at large.

Mrs. Crow sewed night and day to fit out her distinguished husband, in order that he might appear to advantage among those whom they conceived to be stars in the nation's firmament. A tailor was employed to cut and baste. Mrs. Crow piqued herself upon the display of immaculate linen to go abroad, as she had on making a record at home. Sewing machines were not yet in use, and it was no small test of ladyship to stitch by hand the wheel-barrow collar of the prevailing fashion, following a crease as deftly as though it had been a drawn thread on a straight edge. Mrs. Crow was much given to proving her skill by exhibiting her specimens, and she claimed as admirers all who respectfully listened to her self-recitals. She was quite as likely to seize upon a mission to exhort the social leader of the community on the correct way to popularize and "hold up" her family, as to be found rendering a less presumptuous service.

The Hon. Saul Crow felt the need of his capable wife to ingratiate him into his new settings, and he invited her to accompany him on his initial visit to the State Capital. When at length the day arrived for their departure, and the two presented themselves, in their brand-new clothes, before an awed populace, their own family and friends scarcely recognized them. Mr. Crow's collar was stiff and uncomfortable. His conventional beaver was in constant danger of falling off his brow. His satin vest was a standing object of pleasing admiration to them both.

Mrs. Crow appeared with hair mounted high in an experimental coil on the top of her head,

93

rendering the whereabouts of her bonnet uncertain. Her ears, freshly pierced and swollen, were jeweled with long pendent drops, while sundry accessories and furbelows gave *chic* to her toilet. The well-filled satchels underneath the seat of their carriage completed the outfit.

The travelers, to be sure, would have been more comfortable in their usual habiliments, but it would not be expected in persons of their rank, and the ordeal was endured cheerfully for the glory of a less honorable constituency, looking to its representatives to make a record for the county from which they hailed.

Arrived at their destination, the newcomers put up at the most fashionable tavern, and the Hon. Saul Crow inquired immediately for the Governor, stating that he desired audience with His Honor at once, because of a Resolution which he was in haste to introduce. He wished, also, to present his wife, Mrs. Jane Crow, of whom the Governor must have heard. Being advised that the Governor and many of the legislators were stopping at a less pretentious inn, the Crows removed forthwith to the house where the Chief Executive made his headquarters, surrounded by a motley assortment of decidedly plain-looking men. The Hon. Saul Crow was the only one who appeared suitably dressed for his position.

It seemed to Jane Crow that though the Governor's garb was neat and tidy, if *she* had been his wife, she should have taken some pains to have him appear as well as the best. However, Mrs. Crow soon rose to the occasion, pluming herself upon the patent fact that the Hon. Saul made the finest appearance of any member of the legislature, and not even excepting the Governor. And she noted, with excusable pride, that her husband alone, of all these men, had the politeness to extend the courtesies of the convention to his wife.

The name of the newly-elected legislator was dutifully announced to the Governor of the State.

"And who," inquired this dignitary of his secretary, "*who* is this Hon. Saul Crow? I had understood that Jacob Cameron was the people's choice in his district, as many important questions are to come up."

"He is a man of advertised fame and little else to go with it," the secretary explained, "but he is possessed of purpose and wit—just enough to carry him over—while he is bolstered up by the open admiration of his wife, such as other

95

the length of their journey, secretly tucked away in the folds of his shot pouch. Holding it high with outstretched arm, then dropping it into the ground, he vowed:

"Elizabeth, here under these bending skies, amid the blooming of flowers, and the singing of birds, and the hissing of reptiles, and the crawling of creeping things, for better or for worse, I trow thee that by the sweat of my brow this henceforth shall be our home."

Stepping forward and dipping her gourd into the bubbling stream, Elizabeth poured its contents into the open groove in which the acorn lay.

"Jacob," she responded, catching his mood, "in joy or in sorrow, I accept this as our abiding-place, and may our last days not disappoint us in the fruits of our toils and sacrifices."

At this, the acorn was covered and carefully staked about, the tent was pitched, the camp-fire built, and Jacob and Elizabeth Cameron were "at home" to their friends, though surrounded with the solitude of a lonely forest.

Having decided upon the location of their home, Jacob proceeded to fell timber for his cabin. To raise this, it was necessary to scour the country for "hands" living at a distance. But women are wont to keep to themselves, or show forth only in their private cooings. He is said to mean well. If infused with stronger minds, he is quite available."

The legislature had no sooner convened, than Saul Crow perceived that the picture which had intrigued his imagination during the heat of campaign was not likely to materialize. To possess just that degree of consistency of compromise which is often necessary to carry a movement by tact or stealth, measured by steps and degrees, without exciting the contempt of the radical element; and at the same time to maintain that integrity which a just cause deserves—these were perplexing problems confronting the Hon. Saul Crow.

A reform is an easy task, he found, when confined to a popular uprising; but when brought into conflict in legislative halls, faced with the danger of wholesale defeat if launched on an unfavorable sea—then it becomes quite another problem. Saul learned, as have others to their sorrow, that the details of many an outlying future have been planned and dovetailed together by impractical dreamers, rocking themselves and toasting about their home fires. Alas! for theories that seemed faultless, when put to a

THE CROWS IN PROSPERITY

practical test. Often they who least succeed in their own affairs are most confident of their ability to direct the affairs of others, and to administer the public good. The breadth of mind, the tact, and the compass of information which qualify one to view a question from all angles, with the magnanimity and purpose of soul to maintain the general good in ways that do not react unfavorably—these constitute the essential qualifications for the soundest legislative enactment. Looking the ground over critically, the Hon. Saul Crow could find no place to bring in his cherished Resolution, though afterward the opportunity fell in his way to accomplish a greater benefit to the objects of his solicitude by acts of neighborly kindness in excess of the law.

Great changes were wrought in his life through his experiences at the State Capital. Having gained his position by tact in shifting his sails to meet a favorable wind, and with no fitness other than means and facilities for becoming widely known, his brief term of power did little save to disqualify him for settling back into the groove which he felt he had outgrown, while he possessed no qualities for developing growth or promotion in his accidental calling.

Whereas he might have made comfortable livings for his family by remaining at farming and attending to his bees, Saul had lost, instead, not only connections, but interest, as well. From that time forward his life was embittered by want of appreciation on the plane to which he had been raised. It was a question as to what depths of despair his blighted ambition might have carried him, had it not been for the sustaining hand of Mrs. Crow. She took quite as much delight in rehearsing the honors Mr. Crow had once enjoyed, as she had on former occasions in discoursing upon what he was about to achieve.

Thus, after a fashion, the reputation of the family was maintained, though it was too late to overcome the momentum lost by the necessity of beginning anew. In course of time the children married, making homes for their distinguished parents, and it was doubtful if, after all, the honors achieved and magnified by chance, did not afford the Crows more satisfaction and happiness than a fortune could have given them, gained in an undistinguished way.

The Hon. Saul Crow continued to grow in grace as his years increased—in spite of lingering symptoms of vainglory which occasionally cropped out all along his life's career—until at last it was left for Mother Earth to extract the roots of the disease through folds and meshes of the winding sheet.

Martin Terry and His "Daggertype"

AT NO time in the history of pioneer progress was portraiture more popular, or the artist more self-satisfied, than early in its career. It was the forerunner of all that after-school of accomplishments commonly regarded as luxuries, if we except needlework and such other devices as feminine delicacy is wont to invent. Frontier art took rise in portraiture which was customarily wrought in crayon or oil. Its subjects were confined to men of prominence, and a feeling of deference, sometimes amounting to awe, obtained toward him who was counted worthy to become a sitter for a portrait. The modesty of a common folk would have been an object of scrutiny, should he presume to intrude his countenance upon paper, and to appear in the long, straight line of samples suspended from the artist's wall.

Portraiture, as a rule, confined itself to free-hand work—a style which had the advantage of affording the artist great range in the exercises of individuality, by placing within his reach the ability to overcome wrinkles or reduce prominent features to any desired proportion. An artist could eliminate warts and wens and adorn the most pallid cheek with rosy tint; while he was prone to enliven the somber hue of his subject's cloth with crimson or gold. And it was within his legitimate province to shade the cue, which he sometimes did; to deepen the tone of the complexion, and to overcome any insinuation of declining years.

Since hands and feet have ever been regarded by the craft as a difficult study, the artist was thought to have earned his pay when his portrait was declared finished at a stage resembling a man sawed off at the bust. Needless to say, the identity of the subject was open to question, since it was difficult sometimes to believe one's eyes when brought face to face with himself. But an artist who could not argue his case, and bring out the points of resemblance and overcome the prejudice of a customer, had missed his calling.

At a later date, venerable women, such as were esteemed representative of their sex, having retired in honor from the responsibilities of raising their families—these also were considered worthy to be immortalized in portraiture. The approved artist was accustomed to give his lady ideal settings by placing her inside an open window or door, so that she might appear in that negligee which suggests home and rest. He who aptly wrought so divine a conception had transcended his profession, out of the confines of the mechanical, into the realm where breathe the living poet and the philosopher.

The ambrotype and daguerreotype, which followed, brought a marvelous likeness within the reach of all. It was soon after the introduction of these, that Martin Terry found his way to Elizabeth Cameron's door. Seating himself beside her, he begged a private interview, and drawing from the bosom of his roundabout a parcel neatly folded in the soft tanned jacket of some tiny creature of the forest, he unwound the package, keeping close watch of Elizabeth's face, lest, in the twinkling of an eye, he should lose that joy of surprise which he was sure would shine forth in her countenance at the first glimpse of his treasure—a small, black, book-shaped box, closing with hinges, and called a "case" by the craft of the times.

"You couldn't guess in a month who's in here!" Martin began.

102

MARTIN TERRY AND HIS "DAGGERTYPE"

Elizabeth had a faculty for reading prophecy into natural events, and to Martin's great astonishment she guessed it at once.

"Somebody's been tellin' tales out o' school," Martin accused. "I told him plain as I could speak, that we didn't care to have it get out for a spell yet, at least. But bein' it's you, I wouldn't mind to let you into the secret, in particular as I'll have to look to you to set me up in the ways of the world as to comin' events that to all appearances ain't far off neither."

Martin opened the case, and when Elizabeth gazed upon the figures made immortal by this new art of photography, a suppressed smile played over her lips, though she remained speechless till Martin pressed her for the praise which he was sure waited upon her tongue.

"So you have been trying our new artist! Really, you are to be congratulated upon this evidence that Jemima is not ashamed to be found in your company, to say the least."

With satisfying meditation, Elizabeth looked long upon the picture of Jemima Jump and Martin Terry posed with a brace at their heads —their arms protruding from the necks of one another. The figures were so elongated as to suggest a double pipe-stem terminating in a cross.

But whether the novel pose was a blunder through ignorance in adjusting the focus, an accident, or a villainous attempt at ridiculing the unwary, never will be known.

"What do you think of us?" Martin demanded.

"Really, Martin, I must say I like it—that is, for you—but don't you think he got you rather tall?"

"That was my first opinion, Mrs. Cameron, but I'm getting over it now."

"How did you screw your courage up to this point, Martin?"

"Well, it was this way. Ever since I first clapped my eyes on the portrait of Mr. Cameron's mother, I've had a longin' to see Jemima's picture, settin' ca'm and lookin' out at a window—kind o' peaceful; and t'other day I's goin' along the street, and lookin' across, there stood a wagon with a good-sized house on't and a stove-pipe comin' out o' the roof. Just then I met Jemima, and says I, 'Can you see to read the letterin' on the side o' that house?' *She-she,* 'Yes, sir. It says *Secure the shadow ere the substance fades,* and I understand they're makin' pictures there.' Thinks I to myself, 'Martin Terry, now's your chance!' And says I, 'Jemima, if you wouldn't mind sparin' the time to set a few weeks for a picture, here's the

104

chink to pay for it,' says I, clappin' my hand on my wallet. She just started right along in, that minute, and *she-she,* 'I thank you, Mr. Terry, it's very kind o' you. I've always wanted a picture but never felt able to pay for it.'

"I never seen a kinder man than that dagger-type 'Squire, for the minute we entered the door it appeared as though he'd always been acquainted with us, and before we'd been there an hour he told me more about pictures than I ever knew in my life. He was powerful clever, and says he, 'I'll take you both exactly as cheap as one o' you, and I won't ask more'n twenty minutes o' your time, neither.' Says I, ' 'Nough said— it's a bargain!' 'Now,' says he, 'I'm ready. Sit here.' And we wa'n't long a-mindin' him, I can assure you o' that! No sooner had we sot down than he crossed our arms in a way that jus' got me a-thinkin' o' old times, before Jemima went off among the Injens, and just as he disappeared behind a curtain, says he, 'Now you may wink and breathe perfectly natural till I come out. Then you must remain motionless for twenty minutes, not movin' a particle, and I'll show you a picture, the likes o' it hain't never been seen in these parts before. But first, I must know if you want just heads and shoulders or full life

105

size.' Says I, 'We want no halfway work about it, bein's we've bargained for all of us, and if you can't live up to your word, 'Squire, now's your time to back out. The bargain calls for throwin' in the hands and feet, as I understand it, and no extra charge, neither. I want no sawed-off appearance, lookin' as if I'd run out o' means to pay for finishin' the job. No, 'Squire, I know where there's a boss that'll take us—hands, feet and all, by payin' him the difference.' That wound up his bickerin', and he tended to his business."

"Martin, I believe I'd sit again sometime," Elizabeth suggested, "and tell him to make the next one about as stout again, and as short again. I think it will look more like you and satisfy you better."

"I noticed that as soon as I clapped eyes on 'em, and says I, at the time, ' 'Squire, I don't want to hurt your feelin's, but if you'd pare a l-e-e-t-l-e off the length and put it on the breadth, it'd be a good deal more to my likin',' and says he, 'What do you expect, man—only settin' twenty minutes? We can't pare off a daggertype and piece it out nohow. It takes crayon for that. But like as not you'd have to sit a month in that same position for a crayon.' Says I, 'I don't mind the time, one item—not one item do I care, 'Squire, how long it takes, so it comes out to my likin'. And for that matter, it didn't seem five minutes that you's takin' that picture, though I didn't think to time you. Even allowin' for appearances I wouldn't take half I'm wo'th for this picture. The crayon work appears to be a l-e-e-t-l-e better proportioned and peaceful lookin', but the daggertype, 'Squire, has the faculty of gettin' us a great deal more happyfied.'

"Now here's another matter that may surprise you," Martin continued, producing a paper closely resembling a court document, which he proceeded to undouble, his face kindling with fresh emotion as he edged closer.

Elizabeth was surprised and delighted to see a license authorizing Martin Terry to be joined in holy wedlock with ——.

"What does all this mean?" she questioned, with evident gratitude, for really the neighbors were beginning to wish that someone would be raised up to bake and brew for Martin in his own right—with him apparently full-handed and no one to care for him, while Jemima was empty-handed and idle most of her time—a double portion of responsibility to all. But observing a flaw in the papers, Elizabeth called Martin's attention to the fact that his sweetheart's name had been omitted from the document.

"It's this way, Mrs. Cameron. Says I to myself, 'Martin Terry, if you're ever goin' to marry, it's time you's about it!' So I thought I would supprise Jemima by gettin' the license. But when I bargained for 'em, the Judge, says he, 'What's the lady's name?' Says I, 'Don't you think you're pryin' into my private affairs a l-e-e-t-l-e too much, General?' Says he, 'But I must put her name on the license.' Says I, 'I reckon she can sign her own name yet—and for all you know, I may have two or three in tow.' Says he, 'Well, I can't sign my name to any such document till I know the facts.' Then I nettled up, and says I, 'Who's asked you to sign it?—Here's your cash and I want my license. I hain't been dwellin' on this subject these twenty years for nothin'.'

"When he seen that I's in for standin' up to my rights and wa'n't in no frame o' mind to be triflin' about it, he give me up my license. And now I'm on my way to show 'em to Jemima an' have *her* sign it, and I 'low to stay and eat a bite while she's considerin' the question. I'm bound to have a downright plain talk with 'er tonight. If she comes agreeable to the idee, as I've the grounds to think she will, I'll be in for some of

your advice. You're more up with the world, as
to the top o' the fashions, than either of us—and
that's saying no harm o' Jemima, neither. I don't
want no scrub weddin' after waitin' all this time
—that is, if we should be married at home. But
what little I've been lookin' around, since I've
been dwellin' on this matter, I can see that runnin' away to get married appears to be all the
style."

Involuntarily, peals of laughter broke from
Elizabeth. "From whom do you wish to run,
Martin? I think none of the neighbors will op-
pose you."

"Well, *back-ash!* If Mr. Cameron'd lend me
his team, I'd run away to get married, if 'twa'n't
for nothin' else but to outwit the youngsters in a
bellin' scrape. As for treatin' a pa'sel o' ruffi'ns to
pay 'em off for mindin' their own business an'
lettin' peaceable folks that want to enjoy themselves alone, I ain't in for it nohow. And if *she's*
willin', as I think she will be, I wouldn't mind
runnin' away one item—not one item would I
mind it. But I'll be by you again before matters
come to a head, and if you wouldn't mind to be
plannin' for our comfort in the meantime, Martin Terry'll be much obleeged to you."

The prospective bridegroom gathered up his

precious belongings, made his farewells, and waved happily to Elizabeth as he disappeared down the road.

The details of the wedding of Martin and Jemima followed the prevailing custom, even to the costumes of both—the white satin gown of the bride being a gift of the groom. Though Martin was ill at ease in his dickey and stock and wheelbarrow collar, he was well aware that society expected these. Following the happy ceremony, as the guests dispersed with many kind wishes and farewells to Mr. and Mrs. Terry, a shower of rice marked the transit out of the ideal into the real, when, after a long and needless separation, two lives met and ever after moved on together as one.

Under the impetus of his new life, Martin abandoned the chase as a source of revenue, and established himself in trade. He built a tannery, bought and sold hides, and supplied a wide territory from the products of his business. Mrs. Terry proved an efficient helpmeet. She kept her husband's books and carried on his correspondence, since, in his opinion, she was the only person capable of so responsible and scholarly an undertaking. Mrs. Terry was not insensible to

the advantages of wealth, and the mutual benefits arising from sharing the burdens of business
were sufficient to prompt them to labor together.

At first the "drummers" who called were not
inclined to throw off that reserve which is natural with men in the presence of women. While
Mrs. Terry was doubtless a most delightful office
companion to her husband, nevertheless, intuitively the wandering tradesmen formed the
habit of inveigling Martin out behind the store,
where they could "jew" one another and drive
bargains without intrusion.

Mrs. Terry spared no pains, however, to overcome this apparently groundless prejudice. She
donned the calfskin boots and rocked herself on
the front porch of the shop, and otherwise sought
to impress a querulous public that she was of the
same clay as her husband. It was due largely to
the absence of rivalry in his line of business that
the merchant was able to hold his trade at all,
under an innovation so embarrassing.

Having acquired a competency by gaining
upon himself, Martin Terry began to indulge in
conceit. He fancied he was born to a better fortune than to spend his days among neighbors less
given to advancement, and, yielding to the spirit
of the day, he pulled up and moved away, eventu-

ally establishing himself in one of the larger cities of the West, where the Terrys were lost in the whirl of push and progress—not realizing the change that must come to them at a time of life when men reap rather than sow. Thus, after a somewhat eventful career, they became themselves the objects of charity in their age, as the final outcome of a series of successes and failures more or less common to all.

A Glimpse of
Home Life

FROM the day that Elizabeth made over Jacob's bottle-green imported broadcloth wedding coat, that had branded him a "fop" on their first visit among strangers, and remodeled her leghorn bonnet by pressing it over a jug, her aid and advice were sought, that others might also resemble her in fashion of their garments and "pokes." Accordingly, whatsoever was done was a copy of Elizabeth's handiwork; though dints and soil were the only available excuses for "doing over" a bonnet.

Fields of rye were cultivated and women learned to braid and sew the straw, providing hats for the men and boys, as well as for themselves. Their shapely blocks needed no changes from year to year, save as the chief stylist herself set the fashion. Elizabeth's first crude "form" was a contrivance of wood whittled out by Jacob's drawing-knife and polished with a glass scraper; and upon whatsoever he and Elizabeth decided, that became the fashionable mode. When the lathe was introduced a block of more regular proportions was turned, and this was modeled after the bonnet worn into the Settlement by a city visitor, and was, therefore, according to the latest importation. Changes in fashion consisted mainly in modifying or extending the "flare" by splicing the block, in lowering the crown, in arranging ribbons and capes, and sometimes in adding a facing or a frill. Straws were freshened by bleaching with sulphur.

That was a memorable day when Jacob returned from town in great haste, and, giving a kick to the bonnet-block, rolled it out of its accustomed corner, seized his ax and vehemently demolished the seasoned old "walnut knot," saying he had lived over a hod of brimstone for the last time! A new millinery establishment had come to the village, with a window full of bonnets and ribbons and feathers and frills; and even though Elizabeth expostulated that there would be nothing suitable for a dear little old lady for whom Jacob "had a proper regard," he remained adamant to her entreaties.

The first importation of up-to-date headgear was the "Gypsy" with its rounded corners only half concealing the ears. A pair of stems filled

114

with roses graduating from full blown down to buds had been tucked in at the sides. A senseless bonnet it was, with no strings to it, and no pretension to protection against the sun—as useless as it was gay—and it betokened a depravity which called forth the anathemas of the pulpit, where its wearer was openly rebuked on the Lord's Day and accused of appearing like a "calf looking through a rosebush."

Winter brought with it no relief. This colder season developed a bonnet literally covered with feathers and plumes, though none but the most courageous parishioners could withstand the verbal ecclesiastical missiles thrust against the "vain pomp and glory of the world" as personified in the fashionable bonnet. A well-meaning, over-zealous Divine, faithfully discharging his duty as he saw the light, was wont to assure his hearers, with deafening screams, that there was no possible way to hit the heart of a bird save to shoot through the feathers.

So established was the clerical enmity, especially toward flowers and jewelry, that women wearing these devices of Satan were known to have been refused admittance to the semi-confessional of the church. The peace of the community seemed threatened from the day that the

fashionable bonnet was ushered in. This was regarded as a hopeful sign rather than otherwise,
however, the inevitable prelude to purging the
community of its waywardness. It was believed
that the shameful bonnets would be laid aside as
soon as repentance had run its course.

It was but natural that the elderly women
should deplore the passing of their time-honored
serving blocks, but gradually the extremes in
style wore down. A more happy blending of
youth and age was an agreeable compromise,
though the bonnet itself surrendered nothing,
but remained the distinguishing feature of
women's costume.

From the earliest introduction of religious
worship, there was never any very considerable
lapse of time without some Paul to plant, or
Apollo to water, the good seed. Jacob and Elizabeth were among the foremost supporters of the
current minister, whoever he chanced to be, and
their home was the abiding-place for preachers,
colporteurs, school-teachers, and all going-about
persons engaged on errands of mercy or duty.

It fell to Elizabeth's portion to make the com-
munion wine, to bake the unleavened bread, and
to wait upon baptism for all the country roundabout. Immersion was the approved mode, and
116

although Jacob himself had been sprinkled, he had no hesitation in opening his house to those of differing faith. He constructed steps leading to the River's edge, where the services might be conducted under the sheltering branches of the big oak tree. Elizabeth prepared a baptismal robe for the women, that they might not suffer from exposure, upon coming out of the water.

Many attended a Sunday baptism. Even though strangers from a distance, all were made equally welcome, with no question raised as to who they were, or from whence they came. Ample provisions were ever in store for man and beast. Whole families sometimes accompanied the "candidates"; and large crowds were attracted to witness the ordinance, while those who cared to do so, were privileged to remain.

Dressing-rooms were assigned—hastily improvised in off-corners of the rooms; and when the clothesline had been filled with dripping garments left to dry, and all the guests were ready, the feasting began. Not only was there temporal provision, but spiritual blessings were poured out as well, and sometimes shouting mingled with oral prayer, as the outward manifestation of that peace and joy which reigned within. The celebration of "baptism" was an established custom of the times and place, a sort of passover feast, that left in its wake the realization of rest under the sheltering wing of the Abiding Presence. Upon the dispersion of the crowd, Jacob was wont to load down the clergyman's buggy with breadstuffs and sundry eatables, as a slight expression of his gratitude to the minister for bringing the Kingdom of Heaven so near at hand.

This was the work of the day; but night found Jacob and Elizabeth, as usual, at home with their children, in accordance with their conviction to "train up a child in the way he should go," that when he is old, he should not depart from it. So long as the greater inducements of home and family were counted among his privileges, Jacob was not inclined to scattered endeavors bearing little or no relation one to another. It was his thought that a lighthouse, searching about for the lost, absorbed in a moving throng, would be a poor makeshift for safety. To his mind, "letting in the light" was incomparable as a vocation. He was not austere among his children, but entered into their sports with cheer and zest, building for them playhouses and swings, recording their birthday progress on the jamb of an out-of-the-way door, where the height of each was marked and the date affixed with appropriate ceremonies.

The younger members of the family eagerly looked forward to the first snow-fall, for then, as a special treat, they were permitted to "make tracks" with their bare feet in the newly-fallen snow. There was no time-limit restriction to this, nor was one needed, for a brief plunge sufficed to furnish the necessary thrills, and left no untoward effects. Each son, in turn, upon reaching the age of twenty-one years, was presented with a horse, saddle and bridle, and a new "freedom suit" complete, including his first "plug hat." In disposition, the Cameron children were not wanting in that touch of nature which makes the whole world kin. Somewhere between the age of bare snow-feet and the donning of the "freedom suit," there came a "running-off" period, which affected fathers variously, according to their types.

Father Cameron's old friend and neighbor across the River was a weeping prophet who took to "petition." Jacob himself inclined to "prophecy." When involved in the same problems they arrived at the same conclusions, though by different routes. Father Perry's faith led him to "catch hold of the horns of the altar." Father Cameron drew his inspiration from "every beast of the forest is mine, and the cattle upon a thousand hills."

Father Perry wept on his neighbor's shoulder, on learning that their two sons were planning to slip away from the home nests. Father Cameron said, "Let them run! If any of my boys want to leave me, they're the ones I want to be rid of!" And he called his own lad to his side, and presented him with a crisp two-dollar bill, to tide him over till the wanderer should strike a "job." Confronted with the loss of his birthright at twenty-one years, discretion seemed to the young adventurer the better part of valor, and the freedom of the world became as naught in comparison with the loss of a freedom suit.

The venerable fathers little realized that one of them had been made the instrument through which the prayers of the other were answered, so prone were they to the conception of religion as a matter of bargaining with God, rather than the natural relation of cause and effect.

The "Rule of Three" in the Cameron household meant that all should be together at prayer-time, at mealtime, and at bedtime. Notwithstanding the many calls upon Elizabeth, through sickness and sorrow, either she or Jacob remained with the children, so that seldom did the

120

little ones feel themselves alone, or the house without a head.

It was understood that should a minister of the gospel call, it mattered not what his denomination, he was entitled to respect by virtue of his office, and his pastoral solicitude was taken for granted. The children within call were brought before him, the family Bible was placed in his hands, and he was expected to conduct devotions regardless of the time of day. A clergyman's hands laid upon the heads of the flock, became the symbol of a pastoral visitation.

A tutor was sometimes employed, from among the older boys of the school, that the children might keep up with their classes. He studied with them evenings, sitting around the family board after the supper had been cleared away and the chores had been done. Those children who chose to do so, fell into place at the table, all studying at the same time, and the tutor was expected to give assistance as needed. It thus became an object for each one, of his own free accord, to avail himself of this opportunity for preparing his lessons in advance, since this assured time for skating at recess, and for throwing paper-wads during the hours of class. Withal, it was accounted to their credit, as it was commonly reported that the Cameron family always knew their lessons, though seldom seen at their books.

With evenings at study, and days at school—where they carried their dinners in hampers, each child with fried quail as the *pièce de résistance*—the household was reasonably quiet. When at home, the children assisted one another, and, all things considered, the burden of the large family was not so great as it might seem. The joys offset the trials and none felt occasion to murmur or complain. Elizabeth was clever at games, in which she often joined of an evening. Her knitting and sewing were done, as a rule, by the light of tallow dips while others slept. Each child had some particular "chore" assigned in carrying forward the duties of the day. The father and mother, at the head of the household, required the faithful performance of tasks, and a wholesome respect for their dignity and authority commanded obedience.

"Hare-and-hounds" often brought in wild game for the table. "Tending the traps" afforded a revenue for luxuries and gave the boys experience of trade, through disposing of the hides and pelts which they stretched on the barn doors. Diminutive tanneries were constructed upon the hillside, in banks of ashes. The final outcome of

122

these was a stock of whips, neatly braided, finished with "crackers" and placed on the market. Each boy chose his own individual trade, according to his bent, as independently as though he were breasting the world for himself, since the revenue gained in his spare time was his own, for profit or for pleasure. If by fair means one grew richer than another, it was accounted unto him for thrift in driving bargains, or in making a deal —for some were disposed to work while others played, or were employed at their books.

Though none sold his birthright for a mess of pottage, and no Cain slew his brother, there was no magical absence of friction. Elizabeth was too solicitous for the truthfulness of her offspring to press them for full and final explanations, when there was room for strong suspicions, resting upon such testimony as torn garments and scratched faces. She contented herself with looks and words of general disapproval and with cautions concerning the future. When the baby's curly head was crowned with a fascinating bonnet of burdock burrs, necessitating a close shingling of the treasured locks, she had the grace to pass over undesirable explanations, knowing full well that every member of the family would expose his back to a flogging before he would single out one of their number as culprit, since each had a share in the calamity. The chiefship of the clan rested on age, subject to popular favor. That boy who would direct the cook to the hollow stump which contained the Easter eggs of another, was a far way from promotion to leadership in the tribe.

A favorite sport among the boys was cockfighting, which developed into a trained science and branched out into a neighborhood enterprise. It is fair to presume, however, that no mutual understanding concerning the business existed between parents and children—the unsightly appearance of their unplumed fowls being a profound mystery to the unsuspecting mothers.

Musical instruments were not in common use, but jew's-harps, bone clappers and cornstalk fiddles, played by amateurs, rivaled the guitars, fiddles and flutes of the more select artists. The combined volume of all these devices, joining in an improvised concert, at least relieved the surplus energy of the youthful performers, though the sound thereof was far from harmonious.

There were laws of decorum in music, as fixed as the laws of the Medes and Persians. It was an occasion long regretted, when Elizabeth first heard the uncultivated and ill-bred village choir sing a "major" at a funeral, to the accompaniment of the newly introduced chapel organ! None but tunes in "minor" key were considered suitably soothing to a mourner. "Major music" as a dirge was unthinkable. A favorite hymn was that of Isaac Watts:

> *Hark! from the tombs a doleful sound;*
> *My ears, attend the cry;*
> *Ye living men, come view the ground*
> *Where you must shortly lie.*

All members of the Cameron household were possessors of sweet voices, and in their more exalted moods the tuning fork and the oldtime singing book, with its "buckwheat" notes, were brought forth as signals for a family "sing." With Elizabeth's rich alto and Jacob's deep bass, they made a glee club, complete in themselves.

It was no small task to properly clothe so large a family, but each Fall a shoemaker came to the house and measured every member for shoes and boots. Each person in turn stood on a paper, while an outline of his foot was marked in pencil, as a pattern for the soles. These and other measurements were taken to the shop, and the completed shoes when returned filled a large basket.

The not overly devout shoemaker conceived a violent dislike for the two-hour sermons of the local minister, and took it upon himself to remedy the evil. "Jinks! *I'll fix him!*" he vowed. And he signed, as his contribution to the subscription list for the support of the preacher, a fine pair of kipskin boots, made to measure.

The boots were beautiful and the recipient was most grateful and proud to possess footwear of such distinction, and he kept them for Sunday use and pulpit display. Unfortunately a slight mistake had been made in the length. Before the first hour of service was over, the preacher's toes began to pinch, and ere the second hour was more than begun, a look of agony passed over the clergyman's face, as he shifted his weight, first on one foot and then on the other, in a vain effort to gain a little respite from the distressing pain.

The service was noticeably shorter than usual, and as the minister could not well lay aside a rare gift without seeming ungrateful to a generous parishioner, he chose the lesser of two evils and cut short his sermons instead of lengthening his boots.

A GLIMPSE OF HOME LIFE

Once a year the tailor, Mr. Linst, arrived at the Cameron home with his cutting table and goose. There he measured, cut, fitted, and made by hand, suits of clothes for all the men and boys; and no one was without an everyday suit, with a special one for Sundays and festive occasions.

Thanksgiving and Christmas were looked forward to with excited preparation. Roast goose and plum pudding were traditional favorites for the Christmas dinner. These, with a bountiful supply of vegetables and relishes, puddings and pastries, comprised the joyous feast. The fowl, prepared with dressing, was hung before the huge, blazing fireplace, suspended by a hook fastened underneath the mantel-tree. A pan placed below the goose caught the drip with which it was basted frequently, being turned as often, that all portions of the roast might be exposed to the blaze.

Christmas Eve found families sitting in expectant composure, awaiting the arrival of Santa Claus with gifts from his reindeer-land; or Kris Kringle, coming in on all fours, with shaggy coat and flaming tongue, scattering sweetmeats among the little folks, and lapping at the frightened children as they attempted to gather these up.

A belief in ghost-craft was rife among the superstitious who accepted, with favorable allowance, Martin Terry's accounts of his discoveries of hidden resources underneath the soil, as well as Gideon Van Cott's constant apprehension of the dawning of a millennium, the sudden collapse of the world, and the end of time. Nothing is more contagious than the beholding of ghosts. Among the venders of advanced thought were fortune tellers, mesmerists, spiritists, ventriloquists, and those conversant with black art and magic healing generally.

It was not strange that the district school should develop a class skilled in ghost-craft. Little by little the school building came to bear the marks of mysterious visitations. Doors and windows were mutilated; moans and groans issued from unexpected corners; the presence of peculiar mounds, and the fact that there was scarcely a tree on the playgrounds that had not at some time been shredded by lightning, became associated with the unexplained disappearance of an astute lightning-rod salesman, though the more scientifically disposed held to the belief that the earth at this point contained mineral attractions.

The general feeling of unrest, amounting to

an impression of ghostly apparitions, gave rise to the conviction that the place was haunted.

The haunted school-house was at length abandoned—cast off like an outgrown shell that had served its day. Time and decay marked its ruin, and from its foxed sills to its moss-grown eaves, it became uninhabitable for man or beast.

PART TWO

"FAITH OF OUR FATHERS!
LIVING STILL—"

The Onward March

THE stroke of the hammer in the construction of the new school building in the village was the signal for an onward march of progress. Broad halls and spacious playgrounds replaced narrow "entries" and wooded uplands, and marked the passing of the old, dingy, and inefficient "haunted house" of the district school.

Instead of the log barn and other primitive places of worship, churches rose with heaven-aspiring steeples, and bells that called the faithful folk to prayer. Houses, stores and inns were enlarged or rebuilt, and the wayfaring man no longer was an encumbrance upon the private hospitality of those living in the rural sections.

Bridges with stone abutments replaced those improvised of fallen timbers. The "stake-and-rider" gave way to board fences. Gates succeeded bars. Farming implements relieved much of the drudgery of agricultural life, and horses increased the speed over the slow-going ox-team.

Cooking introduced a knowledge of chemistry, and farming began to be studied as a science.

Subsoiling, drainage, and tiling came into use, and brought forth gardens out of submerged acres lying waste. Books, papers and periodicals quickened the intellect, and railroads facilitated commerce, connecting a chain of towns and cities, and giving rise to free intercourse among a scattered people. Newly-established homes sprang up in every direction. Fashion began to dictate and tyrannize. Greater outlying inducements led to adventures abroad in quest of pleasure or gain.

The church and the school, with their various activities, still constituted the only opportunity for display, unless we except such anniversaries as Independence Day, Show Day and the County Fair, where a beau who did not patronize the huckster's stand and accompany his lady at a turn on the merry-go-round, was little esteemed, since it was plain he had undertaken gallantry without the means to carry it through.

Nothing equaled the County Fair for bringing out the Queens of Sheba with camels laden, and the Lydias with their merchandise of purple, and the women of all the country roundabout, with their trappings and laces. Interest

134

would have been lacking, indeed, without the womenfolks. Glee Clubs, with open-air concerts, were a feature of such occasions, and the sweetness of their melody remains to be excelled.

The debate and the literary society were successors of the spelling school and "singing geography" swept the country in a tidal wave. Considerable dexterity was required to quiver around the syllables of some of the foreign names and lengthy capitals, but nothing yet devised has left so indelible an impress. Its only drawback was the necessity of starting at the beginning, with "State of Maine, Augusta, on the Kennebec River," and continuing down the list until the desired haven at length was reached. It was a glad day when the multiplication table was found to be chantable as well, though this, also, was subject to the same limitations. To arrive at eight-times-nine, it was necessary to go through eight-times-one and all the intervening stages.

The jew's-harp gave way to the accordion, the dulcimer, the melodeon, the organ, and later, the piano. Vocal music, in a measure, ceased to be the overflow of exuberant spirits in pleasing song, and became the spoil of experts manipulating combinations of sound for the production of artistic effects. To the birds of the air was rele-

135

gated the distinction of unfettered, natural out-
bursts of praise.

The practice of medicine was promoted to an
art. In the early days of *materia medica,* when
people were practical rather than theoretical,
success was the only diploma that availed a
practitioner, to warrant his calling. "To destroy
bacteria" was an unheard-of term. But if the lo-
tions of the pioneers were inadequate for such
results, modern discoveries in the science are useless.

To administer quinine and ipecac, and calo-
mel and jalap, and various and sundry stuffs, according to prescribed rules, and to collect the
outstanding accounts—therein consisted the sum
of a doctor's success.

To salivate judiciously, producing a drool and
yet preserving the teeth, was a professional pass-
port into the best families of the community.
Nor was it necessary to be a practitioner in good
standing, in order to accomplish "blood-letting."
An ordinary broom-handle to steady the arm,
and a reasonably clean lance, satisfied the sani-
tary requirements for this frequently prescribed
operation; and this, even an unskilled person, if
he were not fainthearted, was capable of perform-
ing.

136

In addition to this desirable "thinning of the blood" each Spring, the whole family was required to drink copiously of sassafras tea for a week or more, reinforced by frequent draughts from the spigot of a barrel of home brew, composed of yeast and spice bush and various herbs. There was always a barrel of cider in the Cameron cellar, for home consumption. When this "worked" it was permitted to become vinegar. Outside the bars of the fence nearest the road, Jacob invariably placed another barrel of cider, with a tin cup, on a wooden sawhorse, for the refreshment of the general public and the passer-by.

A change came over the conduct of the schools in the new era. Bells announced the sessions, instead of a battering of windows with a book. Individual seats with desks supplanted the long bench where pupils sat facing the wall, and where, if one moved, all must rise. The ox-goad and the ferule were banished as modes of punishment. The habit of self-reporting on honor was introduced. Extreme cases of disobedience were treated with banishment, lest the innocent suffer from association with the refractory one; and the absence of the rod was found to reduce its occasions. Growing refinement led to rivalries

137

in deportment, with a noticeable cultivation of a nicety of taste.

Like a John the Baptist crying in the wilderness of Judea, the early-day colporteur, exhorter and evangelist had sped his lone way through unbroken forests of the Middle West. But former things had served their day. The church now became an institution with a more settled purpose. Physical unction no longer was a synonym for spiritual power. Love, joy, peace, long-suffering, had outgrown their kindergarten sense, and instead of being regarded as rewards to a chosen few, for obedience to a series of Divine commands, they were looked upon as motivating forces available to all.

The common school rose to the rank of the former academy, and out of it stepped the youth of the land into college and university.

The Press, and the various agencies for enlightenment, enlarged the scope of mind. "Organizations" of a public nature replaced the neighborhood "bees" and kindly deeds of individual charity. Society became "fashionable"; though perhaps it accomplished a real mission by diverting some from overintensity of mind and the burdensome weight of soul-harrowing "causes."

138

THE ONWARD MARCH

From the dawn of the new day there were comings and goings in the Maumee Valley, till the mind was taxed to keep up with the changes. But for the graves that marked some venerated spot, many who scattered would not have returned to the Mecca of their former years.

A few of the oldtime settlers still remained— among them Jacob and Elizabeth Cameron, who had built their home and reared their family on the original government grant. It was their thought to occupy the goodly land whereunto they had been brought, till called to their home in the skies. The place to them was hallowed ground, believing, as they did, that they had been led by an unseen Hand into a wilderness to be developed; and they rested under the canopy of widespreading branches of their memorial tree, which had sprung from the tiny acorn planted many years before with no thought of leaving its shade till the same Guide should beckon them on.

It was apparent that the little Settlement was but a mote in the midst of a great, surging continent, bursting into power. Already they had lived to see the carrier, the canal and steam pressed into service of man. As complacent, home-loving citizens they were about to settle

down for a long repose in the peace of possession,
which all felt must follow in the wake of so much
progress, when suddenly the sword was sent into
the land—sent not to disturb its rest, but to
broaden its river of peace.

Living up to the best faith they knew, men
and women had prayed for broader views of life,
but they had not specified the terms of such en-
largement. They could not know that the sacrifice of their bravest and best was the price to be
paid for the emancipation of a race.

The shock which followed the call to arms
galvanized into action and emboldened men to
meet the conflict. Farms were decimated for fields
of battle; homes were disrupted; and the current
of social and domestic life was diverted into new
channels. The dark days ahead made common
cause with all hearts, and the tremendous strain
upon the country at large brought many a problem to be solved by the utilization of forces
hitherto unknown. For once, capital and labor
were at peace one with another.

During the period of the Civil War, large responsibilities rested upon the women remaining
at home, who brought to light a reserve of talent,
and evolved a strength unneeded and unrealized
before. Every soldier habitually sent back, for

140

the support of his family, the remuneration received from the Government in addition to his board and clothes. With the general surplus of funds returned to their keeping, women learned to carry on in business, and to conduct municipal affairs in the absence of men. Wives vied in laying up against a future need; and many a man who had been taxed to the utmost to keep the wolf at bay, returned after the war to find his family comfortably housed in a cozy home, the fruit of his wife's toil and sacrifice—though some came not back at all.

The knowledge of the payment each would receive fostered economy; and this, augmented by continuous, systematic earnings, however small, led to thrift among the busy stay-at-homes, occupied with the many tasks at hand—sewing, knitting, scraping lint, packing boxes, and holding fairs. Growing out of the community of spirit, many interests were held in common, and it proceeded from Elizabeth Cameron's heart and mind to enlarge upon her many acts of neighborly kindness by associating the women of the Settlement into a Dorcas Society, such as was popular in neighboring towns.

When at last peace was restored and men returned to their homes, great changes had taken place. To a considerable extent, the business of the country was in the hands of women. Men found themselves guests, if not superfluities, in their own houses. Their army payments had ceased; they had little or no interest remaining in local affairs and nothing with which to employ their time. Scarcely less distressing than war itself were the readjustments that grew out of it. The old order had been cast aside when the plow handle was dropped for the sword.

Women had taken to reading as never before. Keeping alert to the news of the day, their outlook broadened, their interest intensified, and their pulse-beat quickened to the world changes about them. In contrast, homesick men at the front had discovered somewhat the reserve resources of their own talents—their ability to "brew and bake," to sew on buttons, and to live independent of such womanly ministrations.

When the struggle and the danger of warfare were past, some soldiers chose to espouse these newfound talents and to make a profession of such aptitude. A restless atmosphere, vague and unsatisfied, pervaded the country at large. Impelled by necessity to initiate new industries for the development of resources, men shouldered carpetbags in place of knapsacks. Commercial

142

life on the wing replaced the local pack peddler and the huckster. Scores of women felt it needful or preferable to deny themselves the comfort of domestic life, and to provide for themselves alone, rather than to share a husband's uncertain fortune.

By some, it was conceded an achievement that men and women had learned to live independently of one another. But in after years various and sundry crusades were instituted against the evils following in the wake of such progressive individuality.

Fulsome conceits as to that modern life, in comparison with earlier times, were rife. Jacob Cameron was aggrieved, thinking he detected a spirit of ingratitude toward an antecedent generation, fast melting away.

"As well might the fruits of the tree boast over its roots," he said sadly, "as though living were a modern conception that sprang up by its own volition. A chattering parrot, on aërial flight, is in the clutches of the vulture already, in the tragedy of its final display! It will be the death-knell of our nation when *home* as an abiding place, and the *family* as an institution, shall be trampled under foot as things outgrown; and when an excited populace, drunk with tempo-

143

rary success, shall have consumed its reserve powers upon itself, to be followed by the unalterable law of prostration and decay. May the time never come when strangers delve in ashes to exhume the headstones inscribed with a nation's doom: 'Died a natural death.'

"Civilization itself," he argued, "depends upon the preservation of home and family. I read that some nations are taking alarm, lest they become a land without a people. It may be, Elizabeth, that this glorious Yankee Nation of which we are so proud, shall share the fate of predecessors—I cannot say. But my hope is in the light— that it may shine in full splendor upon my country before it is too late."

"Well do I remember," replied Elizabeth, "the early days when we had but to blow the horn, to gather together a troop of our children. I never have known bells to do half the service nor to do it half so well. If the American people have not reverently uncovered their heads in the presence of the *family,* and if they have exalted any shrine above the altar of *home,* and if we are in danger of being succeeded by a less qualified, though more populous, people, it is time to offer ourselves in sacrifice, for the uplift of those following in our wake.

144

THE ONWARD MARCH

"I have been hearing in these latter times, how women are becoming a power in the church and community. They are called by various names —evangelists, missionaries, and deaconesses. Why, Jacob, they are doing precisely what I was accustomed to do among the neighbors. Of course, I was able to do more than these, by your help, and by having a home in which to entertain strangers. It never occurred to me to take credit to myself for neighborly acts that someone must do. I didn't go outside to perform good works, and my face and voice made me welcome without the necessity of a garb for recognition. I knew no better than to do whatsoever my hand found to do, without credentials, and with no commission except that which is enjoined upon all."

"You have been in your best element as a reserve in emergencies. But oh, how times have changed!" Jacob sighed. "I read that even co-education is gaining ground in modern progress."

"Co-education *new*, Jacob? You are the last to fly away on the wings of imagination. Did you ever know a district school that was not co-educational?"

"I mean the after-schools, such as colleges and universities. They say women are proving quite as apt as men in higher branches, and in leading specialties, such as medicine and law, for instance. It is true that some are growing dissatisfied, they know not why, and, like Elijah of old, they are seeking their juniper tree and wishing to die. But why should all grasp at the same fruit with which to enhance the larder? Diversity makes for enjoyment."

"I suppose there is a definite law of limitations, fixed beyond reasonable dispute," Elizabeth agreed.

"I'm not so sure of that, Elizabeth—not so sure. There wasn't an herb that grew within twenty miles, but you knew about it. And always the attic was full of roots and barks for the sick—you were sure to need them before the year was over. More than once you've lifted the children from beds of sickness when physicians had given no hope. It all comes to the same thing. I think you've earned your diploma! You're worth a dozen women of these present days, though all their virtues were combined in one!"

"Women seem to be doing the same things now," said Elizabeth, "but by other methods, to suit a changing age. Some are advocating a return to the simpler manner of living."

"Sometime men will learn the secret of happiness," Jacob responded. "Fame and gold will pass for what they are worth, and life will magnify its comforts. Sometime there may be less hurrying to and fro. We need a more reposeful life."

The same forces that later combined to multiply and extend industries, were in existence from the beginning, Jacob contended, wanting only the strain of necessity to complete their development. Knitting establishments, straw factories, woolen mills, manufactories for ready-made clothing, canning, dyeing, and other enterprises, all took rise in the cabins of the pioneer. Now the products of dairy, garden and farm were prepared outside the home. Men waded swamps and dredged lakes; they multiplied railroads and built steamships; they traveled lands and sailed seas, in search of spices and perfumes to whet the appetite and grace the home.

The esthetic gradually superseded the essential. Art became a field for the connoisseur. Men found themselves on the flood of an ever-widening stream, trending they knew not whither. But the dream was one of delightful hallucinations. They wiped the sweat from their dripping brows and pressed hard on the oar, sighting for some far-off fairy-land, out of the crude and homely

147

life of nature, into a state where naught offends the finer sense, with naught to be controlled or overcome.

"Entertaining" broadened into a feature of social life, diverting the interest from, and sharing the attention formerly given to, the family, whose claims threatened to be secondary to this life and to fields of outlying usefulness. Children were valued in the present tense.

Instead of being the epitome of all trades, the home, under training of its mistress, must needs have servants multiplied, who did her bidding for a wage rather than through love or from a sense of duty. A new series of afflictions resulted, since it is easier to bear and forbear in one's own family than to treat with strangers.

The development of specialties multiplied servants, if it did not increase their efficiency. The constant song of "equality" filled the air— the clamor for "equal rights" for women (that professed leverage for lifting the "weaker vessel" out of her moorings); flying banners in parade, borne aloft in political processions, pledging the uprising of the poor to the downfall of the rich —these all were parts of the prevailing mood which wrought a change in the service of the household at a time when it could least be af-

148

forded by employer or employed. A class accustomed to servitude mistook the nature of its emancipation and felt itself thrust upon a higher social stratum where toil was demeaning.

Men built large and elaborate houses, filled with labor-saving devices to render mechanical service the agent of their domestic relief. The difficulties were increased, rather than diminished. Only one with a liberal education and an enlightened conscience was competent to manage the intricate machinery and to control the forces of steam and hydraulics. The "flat" evolved, and "eating out" was tried as an experiment, which sometimes ripened into a necessity, though it could not altogether solve the problem or take the place of the home.

Many grew rich—largely in proportion to their skill and push in supplying the needs of others. Unfortunates less adequately endowed viewed the picturesque careers of the more prosperous with jealous eye, and their discontent became as dangerous as it was unsatisfying, involving a thousand snares unknown before.

Goaded in the name of progress, ambitious young women in great numbers were constrained to turn their backs upon their parents' cozy homes, and the companionship of family and friends, and to seek the more independent life through self-support, however needless or unsatisfactory might be the sacrifice. Eventually women as breadwinners gained such footing as to justify a reasonable expectation of their continuance in this.

When it was observed that many women could maintain an equal footing with men in some of the trades and callings, if removed from the obligations of home, speculation was rife as to their right to a place in the professions and in public offices. Claim was made for the justice of equal suffrage, on the ground that what all can do equally well, all may do with equal right. It was natural that they who were the ribs of *none* should have desired for themselves recognition according to their gifts and graces.

On the other hand, it was argued that since men were held liable for the protection of home and commonwealth, and subject to the draft in defense of these, women, who were the objects of such protection, should not be privileged to dictate the terms of such service. Until equality of responsibility should be manifest, many men were unwilling to venture upon so romantic a theory of government, especially since they themselves were holden, not only for the civil

150

service at large, but for the execution of law and order in municipalities as well.

Some there were who believed that women in politics would purify the pool, since their morals were recognized as superior to the morals of men; which charge, however innocent of intention, would seem to reflect upon the Maker of all. It was a somewhat unfortunate argument to set forth that woman's influence in the social system passed for naught without suffrage, and at the same time to offer as a chief inducement for it, her moral influence in politics, since that which presumptively had failed in its natural tree was not likely to succeed as a graft.

Men opposed to extending the suffrage contended that the only possible ground of concession was for men to be made the equals of women, since it was impossible for women, in view of the draft, to be equal to men. But if it were assumed that men were as women, then had the sword lost its power and ceased to intimidate, leaving a commonwealth exposed to the caprice of outlying ambitions, and the easy prey of whatever nation might claim her for its spoil on land or on sea.

Many men were unwilling to forge for themselves chains, however golden, in time of peace, to be realized in time of danger. "Women can be helpmeets of men and surrender nothing," they said, "but men cannot become the help-meets of women in government without bond-age, since in men is vested the executive duty and force, and their relation would become servile at once."

Those who took the cause less seriously, quoted the warning of the prophet: "Woe unto the wicked!—As for my people, children are their oppressors, and *women rule over them!* O, my people, they which lead thee cause thee to err, and destroy the way of thy paths."

The "temperance crusade" was conceded to be a great moral reform carried on chiefly by women, but Jacob Cameron insisted this was no new attitude of an advanced day. "No, my young friends," he was wont to say, "I have lived longer than you, and my word for it, women were al-ways up to hiding the jug! Many a harvester came home sober, in consequence. It's nothing new."

Jacob insisted that the temperance problem belongs to Cæsar, and is not a question of reli-gion, though Christians number among his sub-jects. He held that if drunkenness is permitted by law, those responsible for this condition should be held accountable for the results, and that the makers of intoxicants should bear the burden of all which that responsibility entails, to the individual, to his family, and to the state —a principle already recognized in dealing with other catastrophes.

"I shall not be here to manage the new century, Elizabeth," he said. "We have read our titles clear to mansions in the skies. But this I know—the weights that have beset the ages will not yield by might nor by power, but by the entrance of light. A time is coming when men will not be elevated to power because they can mass together the greatest number of votes, however obtained. They will be called to administer public affairs because of fitness to bear such burdens. The trouble of this day is that children have too much liberty. The present times do not produce men who have ripened with age and experience, having remained in retirement for the nobler virtues to mature.

"But all this will be changed when there's more light. Then it will be seen that the most distinguished persons are those all-around men and women, who, because of their symmetrical

153

development, are not distinguished at all. Men have been too concerned with themselves and their personal interests to reason well—and perhaps some have been overanxious that heaven shall monopolize the good."

The Law and
the Gospel

THE younger friends of Jacob Cameron delighted in drawing him into an argument. A group of them often gathered under their favorite tree, to discuss with him questions of Church and State.

"What credit accrues in believing that which cannot be denied without exposing one's lack of understanding?" he said to them one day. "There are fixed laws as unalterable as the natural order of seedtime and harvest. Departure from these laws will undermine any government when folly shall have run its course and borne its fruits. Fundamental principles cannot be interdicted. Neither Church nor State can run counter to these laws without suffering the consequences. Legitimate changes will occur in the policies of the Church, but it will still remain a church, fed by the waters of life. Its mission is *from everlasting to everlasting*. God engages himself, but He never interdicts His own decrees.

Take, for instance, a call to the ministry. This must be interpreted in accordance with natural aptitudes, if it is to be authoritative, since theological truth cannot overcome a physiological fact.—But I am breaking a hobby-colt that belongs in another's pasture!"

"What about the prophecy of a day when swords shall be beaten into plowshares, and the nations shall learn war no more?" asked the young theologue.

"That would seem to point to a time," said Jacob, "when petition shall have the force of persuasion, rather than arms. Unfortunately, under existing conditions, the peace-loving are in danger of becoming lethargic in rendering unto Cæsar his dues, expressed in their votes. It sometimes happens that theirs is the fault of poor government, since bad minorities expressed take precedence over good majorities unexpressed. This is the root and herb of much bitterness and leads to many a spasmodic revolt, too late to remedy the evil. Every campaign emphasizes the fact that it takes a disturbed season to bring out a full vote."

"Suppose we do away with wars, and adjust difficulties by arbitration," suggested a political aspirant.

"That may settle misunderstandings of a neighborhood character, where many interests are held in common, and all parties can be made to see alike. But *enforced* arbitration can never obtain in a *free* country, since, by its own definition, arbitration means *to arbitrate;* which, if accomplished, would, in effect, result in a tendency toward dictatorship. Arbitration would not *en*-franchise men, it would *dis*-franchise them, subjecting them to concentration of power, vested in a few exposed to temptation. This is placing too much power in a few little fists. It was to escape such danger and to institute true self-government, that our forefathers established a republic.

"Any considerable departure toward the enforcement of arbitration would be a step in the direction of dictatorship, as I said. Moreover, how can one arbitrate with known enemies and disturbers of the common good? When the police can be disarmed with safety, and the innocent remain secure, it will, in my judgment, be time to risk arbitration and surrender to this wild hallucination. But not until we can dispense with these safeguards, and with the services of the militia and navy, will men vote to disfranchise themselves to accommodate the

157

caprice of the dissatisfied. *There is a way that seemeth good, but the end thereof is bitterness.*

"The strength of appeal is the sword. A foreigner, though his property pays its proportion of taxes, cannot vote unless he is naturalized, simply because he cannot be drafted to defend his vote, if contested. Otherwise, though not eligible to the draft, it might be possible for him to hold a balance of power to make laws in favor of foreign countries whose subjects are eligible to fight, while he, himself, remained secure and removed from the restraining poise of responsibility. Such a mistake would be a dangerous experiment, and might lead to the impairing of the balance wheel. The right of petition affords opportunity to express opinions, which is the sum of all votes, when divested of the executive feature. I never have seen any good come of usurpation."

"Here's one of our industrious naturalized citizens, coming up the road," observed the politician. "Perhaps he'll use his influence to win me votes for the legislature."

"Good day, Pat," called Jacob. "Our young friend here is a candidate for congressional honors, and he's seeking votes."

158

"Sure, sor, and what might you be afther doin' if you once get there?" inquired Pat.

The candidate explained his purpose briefly, and asked, "Do I make that plain?"

"Indade, sor," said Pat, "that's all the throuble! I can understhand that with half an eye open. If you've got any principles to be a-sthandin' up for, that I can't see through, bring 'em out, an' there's nobody in the wide world I'd be afther gettin' votes for so likely as yourself."

The candidate obligingly tacked about, and engaged to mystify that which he had labored so studiously to make plain.

"Now you're a-spakin' it, sor! It begins to sound like larnin', and I'm the last son of Erin to be comin' to America and stoutin' out agin' larnin'. 'Tis a curious counthry you've got, sor. I doubt the likes of it ever was seen. Anybody that's a notion to get dissatisfied can kick up a dale of a row, and by a few tricks, when honest men are aslape, he can get things a-goin' his own way, sor. It bates all!

"But 'tis a good counthry for helping a man to improve to his own likings. When I come over, there was a Tim Maginnis come over in the same

159

boat, in the steerage. I've always known Tim, and a more ginerous sowl never lived. He always threated himself poor and his wife a beggar. He must always be a-givin' away something, or die a-tryin' it!

"Tim conthrived to get on the town council where he came to live at, and there he was at his best, for it only took *one*, to lop over and make a majority; and Tim, he was that plased to find he had more power than the mayor himself!

"And it wasn't like the ginerous man he was, not to be givin' a silk dhress to his wife who had suffered so much on his account, out of the first money he got to place over an improvement. Good sowl that he was! He was niver so happy as whin givin' somethin' away, but this was the first toime in his life he ever had anything to give!"

"A fortunate friend, indeed! Not many of us who have always lived here have his privileges," said the candidate.

"He was indade that! And if you'll sthick to your last principles, a gentleman of your quality and larnin' can sure get a thousand votes, sor, if only you've got the darin' to sthrike out for 'em.

"I was about to tell you, sor, that before the summer was out, Tim was for giving away ivery

160

strate in the town for a railroad, saving only the principal strate, and Tim he was a-conthrivin' a canal, with stameboats sailin' up and down. Then there set up a power of a fuss! Iverybody said 'twas in the heart of the government to make highways for teams and for farmers and such, for to be haulin' their goods to market. and for women and children to be safe in dhrivin' about town, and for cripples and ould folks to be crossing the strates.

"I've heard a dale of this wonderful counthry —how it takes foive years and more and then a foreigner only begins to understhand your government. And Tim, he wasn't for doin' the schmall thing, and voting for something he could see through plain as day, when there was a world of improvements out of reach of his understhanding! 'Twas that way he come to be after getting the votes. It's shore to make throuble to be voting for schames anyone can see through, and there's a dale of a row at the Works on laws, because they can see through 'em plain as day, for the boss he gets all the money, and the hands, they get all the work, and any fool can see through that!"

"Exactly so," said Jacob.

"Well, some got bastely mad at Tim, as

though his wife hadn't as good right to a silk dhress as any ither woman. But Tim, he had no notion to shake off American ways before he'd fairly got into 'em—with all of us standin' by and bracin' him up—and faith, they got into a dale of a fuss! That's why I ain't for voting for anybody that can't work schames that the people aren't afther seeing through with half an eye open—it's shure to make throuble in the end.

"But 'twas the people come out the little end of the horn, with Tim. The joke shore was on thim when they found the rights on their own business had all been given away. Tim, he was too smart not to be found voting for public improvements, as long as the weeds by the roadside and the rails on the fences measured as much front as the castles of the mabobs—and indade, this was the very thing that pulled him through in spite of the people."

"But would the road pay as a business proposition?"

"Now you're spakin' it! You may be sure Tim he was not worsted on his part of the bargain. But as for the stameboats, the lawyers proved the shortage for water, and he had to go back to his first principles and make it a railroad, afther all his throuble! And that's where the weeds and the rails was of great service to him in pullin' him through. The failure come when the people refused to be doin' the ridin'. And the throuble was all in seeing through the schame that Tim was pleased to make for the improvement of his neighbors. This is a wonderful counthry, sor, when a poor man can have the privileges of a lord, and the rich man has no rights in bossing his own business to his liking, with the lawyers a-taking his part. Of all the disturbers of the pace of the counthry, the lawyers are the very worst—and nary a bit of allowance do they make for the very prastes!"

"How did your friend come into possession of means to come over to this country?" asked the theological student.

" 'Twas no thrick at all, sor. Tim he was willin' for earnin' money, but better by far for sphendin' it, like the ginerous creature he was."

"He couldn't get ahead very fast at that rate!"

"Indeed, your honor, Tim he was after seein' through the banking business with half an eye open, and the bankers gettin' rich as lords, by dhroppin' their money into the safes and lockin' out the thaves."

163

"In this country a great deal of the banker's success depends upon public confidence in ability to pay."

"Faith, and that's why Tim he was for runnin' his own business without any thanks to the public. The joke was sure to be on the mabobs, when Tim he was afther gettin' a bank of his own, and a-lookin' out for Tim Maginnis himself. Afther that he had shillin's in great abundance, and his wife so proud as a queen to be a-helpin' him to kape it. She even put in her smoke money to help make him rich. And it just happened that way on Tim's account, that the more money he had in his bank, the less shillin's he had in his pocket, to be a-dhrinkin' himself and a-treatin' of others. It turned around, sor, that the joke was on Tim, when he found he'd been dhrinkin' up shillin's by the ton, for washin' down his bread by the pound; and when he opened his bank, there he was, rich as a lord— and niver a lawyer to pay for fixin' up his principles! And now, Tim he's always in luck."

"Do you think it fair that a rich man should have no rights another is bound to respect?" Jacob asked.

"Now you're spakin' it agin, sor! It takes your honor to be thinkin' up ways just above me

164

reach, but there's one thing I'm sure—it ain't the bosses alone that's gettin' rich. Last wake I wint to a concert in the city to listen to a man with a musical instrument and it beat all how that fiddler did play! And he couldn't spake a word of English, 'twas said. He played for two hours—and would you believe it?—that thafe wint away with *two thousand dollars* in his pockets! And the ushers that sated the people had only a bare livin', and nary a couple of hundred dollars did he place in their hands—and they givin' him sich a ginerous crowd! Nobody has any business with two thousand dollars for two hours of play—'tis a free counthry!"

"But there's a way for an usher to get even with the musician. He can pay him back in his own coin."

"Sure, sor, would you mind a-tellin' me how, and I'll be doin' the ginerous thing by lettin' him know about it—and it might be the same as to do a little for myself in the bargain."

"The next time that great musician comes to the city, let him tend the door, and let the usher make the music."

"Faith, your honor, and who'd be a-goin' to a concert to hear a man play that didn't know a fiddle from a bagpipe? And a dale of a fortune

HOOF-BEATEN TRAILS

would a musician make as a doorkaper! Your plan, sor, would make paupers of 'em both!"

"Then it must be that the musician is getting back some reward for the time and expense spent in so developing his genius as to draw large audiences—in this ability consists his fortune."

"And pray, sor, what might a genius be? I never heard of one in Cork. Is it the same as to be great?"

"A genius is one whose gifts and graces sometimes run in one direction, at the expense of others. It sometimes happens that a genius needs a practical man to take care of both himself and his fortune, after he has earned it. One who is born that way might as well accept the situation gracefully and serve his generation accordingly," said Jacob.

"Indade, if the musician is born to his luck, and the doorkeeper isn't, whose fault is it, and what business has a man getting rich as a lord, for something nobody can help? All the more should a man that's gettin' rich pity the other's misfortunes, and not be a-hurtin' his feelin's by not givin' him a couple o' hundred dollars or such, to make it even."

"How would you prevent the great musician

from making money, since so many people are willing to pay to hear him?"

"Really, sor, it's with your honor to figure out a schame. But what I say is this—that a man has no business with two thousand dollars for a couple of hours' play. It might be a good plan to send in, say, a couple of hundred people at a time to hear him, and so let the baste have a chance to be earnin' his money, as poor people are obliged to do. And that would give the doorkaper a power of a job, in the bargain. At least, that's the way they're talkin' it at the Works."

"Did you feel that you had paid too much for your concert?"

"Niver a bit, sor! If it had cost twice as much I'd still have been ahead, sor! There's a mighty pretty little creature goin' around the counthry singin' like a bird. 'Tis said she's so rich she can't count her fortune, but I'd be the last to stop the mouth of such a warbler, for it's in my heart that all the world should hear her. Nobody cares how much *she* makes—that's the beauty of bein' a woman!"

"You'd favor giving votes to women, then?" asked the politician.

"There's this to be said for it. It gives a man

two chances to one to bate the boss. But if it's the same as to be a takin' of their own parts, and of comin' to blows, I'm not the man to be votin' a black eye onto any woman! I'd rather see the pretty creatures keep singin' like the birds, even if it's the same as to get all the money out of the earth and into their own hands. If you've got any principles on that subject, fix 'em up so the people can't search 'em out, and ivery mither's son of us'll be afther votin' for you. But if the lawyers see through your schame, it's a chance if ye'll bate or get bate!"

"I've often wondered," said Jacob kindly, "how a man feels who arrives in this country a stranger, where he hears a language he cannot understand, and why so many foreigners come."

"Indade, Mr. Cameron, it's this way. When a man comes over from the ould counthry, he has plans of his own in his head. He expects to find people aslape and at peace, and a chance to do as he plases. But he no sooner lights on your wharfs than the throuble begins. And by the time he has been detained for his character, and shmoked for his shmallpox, and turned loose in a strange land without an extra shillin', he does well that he don't go to stalin' from the start. If 'twa'nt for the blessed women folks a-meetin' our wives an' children, and keepin' 'em out of the hands of sthrangers, a-warmin' 'em and feedin' 'em, I don't know what would become of some of 'em. But I must be about my work—already I've been stayin' over-long. Good day, sor; good day!"

The laborer shouldered his toolkit and departed. At length Jacob, returning to his favorite subject, said thoughtfully:

"Voting is not the remedy for the ills of life— such is but a passing delusion. It is a misguided hope to count on the massing together of malleable majorities; there is danger that men may be found undermining their tears by their vote. Our government must not rest on inflation of the ballot for its legislative strength, any more than upon inflation of the currency as a financial system. And men cannot legislate the country into happiness, nor invade the sanctity of the home. The ear of the Lord is not grown dull, that He cannot hear His people's call. If lawgivers are casting about for a short-cut to the well-being of the nation, which will take no account of the moral law, they will search in vain and wind up in despair. There will always be trouble if the State diverts from its significance by treating marriage as of incidental concern,

169

subject to local regulation according to political caprice.

"As for the family—it is the heavenly world-stuff in its crude state; and to suspend it for any reason, for half a century, would rob heaven and impoverish earth. It is the dream of poets—woman on her pedestal—but I do not find her. I have seen a weary woman with a teething, fretful baby in her arms, and a double portion of sorrow and strife. To me, she is a queen enthroned. The glory of a man is one thing, the glory of a woman another, and the glory of a child, still another. Each in its place, they form a perfect trinity. Mutual dependence begets mutual interest, and childhood is doing much to hold the world in poise.

"A popular prejudice exists, which associates the moral law with the saddlebags; and some have come to shy of it, lest, in an unwary moment, they find themselves headed in the direction of everlasting life—as though morality were a scheme to take undue advantage of a man, to save his soul and rush him into heaven without a chance for a hearing! By some the least insinuation of the moral law is resented. Let me comfort any who may be suffering in this wise, by assur-

170

ing them that the civil law takes no one to heaven, but is given for regulation of conduct in the present life. The civil law has discharged its mission when it locates a criminal and brands him with the signet of justice. If it goes beyond this, and attempts to regulate the moral law from whence it proceeds, it transcends its rights, to the increasing of disorder and lawlessness rather than to the abating of them.

"It will simplify the administration of justice greatly, when men come to understand this—as they will when they have stumbled long enough in darkness. And when our souls are saved in Heaven, it will be through no law whatever, for it is a spiritual *family* into which souls are *born*, not legislated, wherein consists a universal privilege. You need give yourself no uneasiness about trapping people into a future inheritance against their wills, should the moral law become the code of the state.

"But I fear I have lived too long in the chrysalis of the past. I have given you the law and the gospel as an old man sees it, looking backward. It is the privilege and the duty of you younger men to interpret life in the light of the present day, looking forward. Each generation must

171

fight out its own problems. There is a favorite
-✗ proverb: *If you want good apples, look for the
tree that has the clubs under it.* I shall expect to
find you there."

Capital and Labor

"I HAVE been spared to see the comings or goings of four generations," said Jacob, in his later
years. "But the children of the King never die.
They outgrow flesh and blood, and then move
to a higher plane. Men cannot be trusted with
continuous power, with all their natures in full
force. Many a Moses has been taken away in sight
of his promised land. Few who toil for its de-
liverance have been allowed to enter in. God will
have no rivals among the children of men.

"The world heaves along in seesaw measure,
with ups and downs. Perhaps it will rise again to
a loftier conception of the family and the life
held in common, for a land without a people is
not a nation. There is room to raise the inquiry
if it be not true that America, in the name of
progress, is developing a crop of ministering
angels for her more prolific successors, who, in
multiplying, will claim the promise of the earth.
Everyone may judge these matters for himself,

173

but it rebukes my practical judgment to admit that all things work to the survival of the fittest. This broad continent never was meant for the monopoly of a minority, either in wealth, in numbers, or in continuous power. The sickle of time is thrust in to avert an evil more often than we know.

"Some contend that an aristocracy of wealth may grow up in this country, and that the poor will be oppressed by such aggregation of power. I do not fear this. What matter to us if railroads and canals be owned by one man, or five hundred men? Whichever way we best are served—that is our gain; only so the resources of the country be not locked up in monopoly. Therein alone is the danger, rather than in expansion, which will furnish employment to many who could not furnish employment for themselves.

"Some men have financial tact to multiply resources; some have educational perception or scientific aptness; others, gifts for the massing of historical facts; and still others, for expounding theology. It is the old story of the body with many members. It would be about as logical to slay the historians, the educators, the theologians, on account of their semblance of leadership, as to upbraid the rich for espousing the develop-

174

ment of public thoroughfares and large industries, which make for the support and employment of those to whom these necessities would not otherwise be available.

"The fact is, we need the rich as much as they need us. I do not see how the country could be developed without them. If the rich prove lenient in deal, it should be accounted a virtue. This modern notion that if somebody has money, another who chances to have knowledge of it, is entitled to a portion, without earning it, is a misconception. Nor should we measure all by pounds and pence. These are the mill, and not the grist.

"As for fortunes, these accumulations are dissipated through natural inheritance in a very few generations. The history of the world furnishes few examples to the contrary. This is just the modern, and I think the better way, of distributing private wealth—a result that was accomplished in olden times by the 'year of jubilee.' Now, Cain and Abel meet, midway on the ladder of fame, only to exchange banners in passing, and move on to untried fields."

Jacob visioned a day when public highways would be paved; when prisoners, instead of working in competition with trade, would be employed on country roads, with portable houses for shelter; when electricity would solve the problems of light, fuel and transit; when dwellers in overcrowded cities would find homes in the country; and the bartering of family supplies would be carried on at every man's door.

"Farming is half a century belated," he declared to his young friends, grouped about him. "But I see this future fulfillment coming. Then livings will not be sharply contrasted, and social opportunities will be enhanced. Outlays for subsistence will be reduced to a minimum, since plowing will be done by electricity, and rail transportation will be less expensive than teams, in the days ahead. Taxation on the property of the moneyed class is already bringing accomplishments to the homes of all. Lawmakers are compelling our youth to become educated, and there is a growing aristocracy of learning."

Jacob paused a moment, lost in his thoughts. "I look around me," he said at length, "and find so many are now gone—and I sometimes wonder if our Heavenly Father is not taking great pains with our mansions in the skies—he is leaving us here so long. And for all our strength is failing, I feel the conscious presence of a Master Being in my soul. It must be my other self. This body

176

must be ripe with years and ready to be folded about and laid aside.

"Oh that I could have lived to begin a career in days of opportunity such as these! But mark my word—the most useful man of the coming century will be that one, whether rich or poor, who least magnifies wealth as a leading factor in happiness; he who practices the gospel of contentment with wages; and who tramples not on the rights of his fellowman. Among the evils to be averted are these: undue haste to get rich; abnormal and distorted conceptions of one's own rights, with a lack of regard for the rights of others; the following after *crazes* that are startling and new, with contempt for standard usages, established and tried; the love of display, of public applause; the fascination of great crowds and thronged thoroughfares, with opportunities to do evil, and light appreciation of the good. All these make for instability, and leave the basic plank of the social structure trembling in the balance.

"To be sure, estimates are sometimes fictitious and misleading. To be unhappy is not the substance of sacrifice, nor is to be happy the proof of useless living. It would be impossible to arrive at a correct census, either of contentment or of real happiness. Our commonwealth is interwoven and held in poise by a network of happy homes, too sacred to be exposed to the gaze of a curious world. When shall we come to understand that it is super-excellence just to be normal—and that to be *usual* is to be great?

"We seem to be passing through the narrows of progress, wherein it counts for a mission to reach a helping hand to tide people over the so-called lower level of life. The time will come, my friends, when fathers and mothers will not find it necessary to wander about, pilgrims and strangers on errands of mercy, or in search of bread; neither will the enjoyments of the family be confined to their own hearthstones, but such pleasures as opportunity affords will be enjoyed together—enhanced because of separate working environments."

"Is it vain, Mr. Cameron, to hope for a more equitable division of the wealth of the world?" interrupted a social reformer.

"*How?*" inquired Jacob, cupping his ear with his hand.

"It is my theory that churches should hold all things in common, the rich dividing with the poor, as did the early Christians."

"That might have been desirable," Jacob ad-

178

mitted, "at a certain time and place, with a certain few, for a certain purpose. But nowhere do I find it intimated as of universal application. All such benefits are acts of love, rather than fulfillment of obligation. What gain is there in burdening the church with such worldly weights, and diverting it from its true significance as the light of the world? Consolidations of the type you suggest are in the nature of business, and usurpation of power is no more worthy in one instance than in the other. It is as unfair to exercise business in another's voice, as to hold voice in another's business. To mass wealth, and then control it, is certainly no worse than first to control another's wealth, in order to mass some of it for one's self. Which of these violates Christian ethics, I leave you to decide.

"I have observed that among those holding such views as you propose, each man starts with himself as the basis of poverty. And while those richer than he should divide with colleagues of his own rank, the proponent sees reasons in abundance why he, himself, should not feel called upon to share with his fellow-craftsmen of lesser income. Probably the best test of such a reform would be for a few like-minded to practice the virtue they preach, that others may behold its beauty and utility; though in my judgment the church would be offering only the inducement of loaves and fishes, instead of the bread of life."

"But, Mr. Cameron, can the sin of covetousness be regulated?"

"I have noticed that when covetousness is denounced from the pulpit, if there is a rich man in the congregation, all eyes are upon him, as though he were a criminal in the clutches of the law; whereas the facts may be that, unwittingly, the congregation, and not the man of means, is exposing its own guilt by its manifest longings. Poverty tests covetousness no less than riches, and should lead to constant self-examination. A courteous foreigner noted this attitude when he remarked: 'Our people are so different from yours. In my country, if one has good fortune, everybody is so *glad*. But in your country, if one has good luck, everybody is so *mad!*'

"Many labor troubles find their pivot at this point, and the church should be careful and clear, leaving no unguarded doors. It is not always the man who has money, who most covets; it may be the man who wishes wealth, but has it not. The sin is not in the money, but in the propensity to desire that which belongs to another. Ample means, many times, induce generosity. The sums given by the rich in secret, that they may seem not to boast, often exceed their known charities. How thankful one should be for the distribution of wealth through luxurious living—giving employment to many, with opportunity to earn their daily bread. A thousand times better than to have distributed the amount in alms, leaving the workers in idleness. That is not selfishness, but benefaction. People need beware, lest in their solicitude for the unfortunate, wrong models be set up, and covetousness be disseminated as a virtue, to be weeded out by the state."

"Do you not think, Mr. Cameron, that the elegance of church edifices in these days has much to do in separating the rich and the poor in their worship?"

"I hardly think so, for I have discovered that the religious impulse elevates. The finest of church buildings have appeal for the most lowly, though they be but just redeemed from the gutter. Streets of gold are their inheritance thenceforth, and they feel to know it. It is a worthy motive to build imposing Sabbath homes, even among the poor. Why should they be content with adobe? There is some grain of truth, perhaps, in the idea of Christianity stooping to conquer. That is well, yet it tells but half the story; for stooping can be utterly unavailing unless met by a religion of rising; though it is most unfair to charge against Christianity, that it does not reach such as are determined not to rise in the scale of moral worth. Such must be amenable to the State. The State crucifies, but the Church resurrects. *'Thou shalt not'* clears the way— *'thou shalt'* goes forward.

"Many have felt that the church should turn out in arms against the evils of the world. I am wondering if this be true. Some Moses doubtless will yet arise, to lead his people, but this should be done in an orthodox way. We gain nothing by adopting one evil to remove another. We already have laws designed for the suppression of wrongdoing; but may it not be that we have failed to consider the importance of making good conduct an object. In courts of justice it is the *law* and not the *criminal* that is tried. If the law covers the case in question, it is adequate. If not, then is the law subject to amendment."

"You have a remedy, then, Mr. Cameron?"

"Call it rather a plan for experimentation. I have fancied it might be possible to provide islands of banishment, where those who are of the

182

criminal class could be quarantined away from the law-abiding citizens. Such a reform measure would meet with general approval, in my opinion, and might be made self-supporting by the development of industries under normal living conditions, and under competent supervision.

"Those who are a charge on the public and a menace when at large, might better fight among themselves, if fight and quarrel they must, than to place in jeopardy the lives of innocent victims. In my judgment it would be a far severer test of a vicious man's courage to be obliged to face the consequences of his acts, shut off from any save dangerous companionship, than to be accorded safety behind prison bars.

"There is no claim upon the government to Christianize these felons, but to control them. That task, the church, no doubt, if obstructions to reformatory and elevating influences are removed, would accept as missionary opportunity. I think the plan might be relied upon to work itself out. At least it might be worthy of trial. It avails nothing to become frantic because a door will not open with a key that does not fit. Get the conditions right, and a way out of our difficulties may be disclosed.

"The Lord has need to shift the sails many

183

times, in order to bring us into favorable angles where He can reach us. If we permit ourselves to grow impatient and distrustful concerning the winds, the sails, and the overlong and tedious voyage, we may strand ourselves and miss the end sought in gaining a port. There is abundant opportunity for the exercise of the functions both of church and state, but the world will wait in vain for a time when it can get along without a Redeemer."

The Scroll of
Memory

JACOB and Elizabeth again sat alone. It was the anniversary of their wedding day, and Elizabeth's thoughts were of the past, as she leaned forward upon her elbows and braided her fingers together while the scroll of memory unfolded before her.

"If it were all to do over again, Jacob, I do not see where we could better it—though I must say we prepared for a life of which we little dreamed."

"Yes," Jacob responded, "I've thought of it much, of late. It is a blessed comfort that a Hand covers all but a day at a time. If this were not so, *the burden of the valley of vision* would have crushed us utterly, I fear."

"Had we foreseen, at the beginning of our journey, all that we since have passed through," Elizabeth agreed, "we should have lost courage. But the joy and the gain have more than recompensed us for the sorrow and the toil—and there is still the future in store. So often we have been at the end of our strength, and compelled by our helplessness to realize our dependence on a Higher Power. We have learned in the school of experience to fall in with the ways that are above our ways, and the thoughts that are above our thoughts. It seems that doors have been opened before us."

"Many a time, when watching the laborers following the plow, I've wondered why bread doesn't grow in place of thistles, that it might be plucked in passing," said Jacob. "Some hold that through violation of physical laws, it was decreed that bread should be won by the sweat of man's brow—though I reckon there's no atoning virtue in sweat."

"If bread grew upon thistle-stalks, to be plucked in passing by," Elizabeth answered, "I scarcely know how a family could be held together. With no necessity for assembling and no incentive to wholesome industry, each individual would wander off at will, and no affectionate gratitude would spring from mutual dependence one upon another. I scarcely see how it would be possible to cultivate the Christian virtues without these incentives."

"You have earned full measure of gratitude,"

186

said Jacob. "Do you remember the day when I jokingly offered you a lifelong occupation, with no responsibility but to preside over a home for two—with yourself for one, and myself for the other?"

"I was thinking of this when you spoke, Jacob. And since that time I have reared nine children and buried two. I have made a true home, for them and for you. There are countless things I do not recall, but I have sat up with the sick and the dying; have laid out the dead and made shrouds; and have worked hand in hand with physician and preacher. I have fed the hungry, and clothed the needy; and waited upon baptism, and enlightened seekers; comforted mourners and entertained strangers. I wonder now how I ever lived through it all!"

"I, too, have been reviewing the past," Jacob confessed. "Have you noticed that most of the old neighbors are gone? The burying ground is filling with their children and their children's children. I have been staking around our family lot, to keep a place for us when our time shall come—and surely it can't be far away. It would be unbearably lonely here but for you. I have been settling my affairs and making ready to leave. So far as I know, I am square with the world—all but that little account with you! And now, if you'll make out your statement, I'll cancel that obligation, and scatter the balance among our children. Then I shall be ready to answer my call when it comes."

"But you, too, have labored, Jacob. You must consider all your toil and sacrifice."

"That was not in the bargain. According to my reckoning, on the terms I offered, with interest compounded for sixty-five years, I owe you more than you can guess. However, just for satisfaction, I have been checking over my own activities, though most of the little things have slipped my mind. I seem to have been busy, for the most part, but I have kept so little record of it all that memory fails. Yet I have held one or more offices of public trust in the community much of the time; and I have given support to the school and the church and the government through all these years, as a public-spirited citizen should. There is a little more I wish to set in order—and then my work is done. But first, I must square my account with you."

"You couldn't pay me off in houses and lands," Elizabeth declared, "if they were fenced with gold! I am looking for my reward to Him who has watched over my life—according to a private understanding we have had from the beginning. No, Jacob, I have been working *with* you, but not *for* you. Nothing short of a mansion in the skies will satisfy me as an inheritance. That will suffice—if I may share it with you. Such consideration has dignified my toil, with no mercenary end in view. Who knows but that we may have been *workers together with God* in this world, and that, if it be His will, we may depart together, to rise from a common tomb on the resurrection morn?"

Prompted by a sudden impulse, Elizabeth rose from her chair, steadying herself with her cane, as she quietly slipped through the open door, alone, and turned her steps toward the near-by city of their dead.

Entering the burial-ground, and feeling her way along the graveled path, she moved slowly about, separating the tall grass which had gained a foothold among the neglected graves. She strained her dim eyes in a fruitless endeavor to read the inscriptions on the many headstones of those who were dear to her. Presently she came to a tall and massive monument with two central figures, surrounded by little mounds. Here slept her sister Deborah, with her gallant young soldier husband, and their children. The better

189

qualities of Deborah's husband had been magnified in funeral eulogies, and the mantle of charity covered his human frailties. No pains had been spared to mark in fitting manner the spot of his last resting place.

Elizabeth paused before the imposing shaft, and stood transfixed against a twilight sky. Involuntarily she raised her eyes to Heaven, and seemed to see, bending above her, a halo of human forms. Paul, the first-born of Jacob and Elizabeth, was there; and near him, her sister Deborah, with her little ones about her, forming the lily-work in the cloud of her vision. Whether in the body or out of the body, she could not tell, but, lifting welcoming arms to them, Elizabeth sank to her knees.

There came a ripple, as of a passing wind. The cloud mist wavered—and she found herself kneeling before the monument alone.

Leaving the burial-ground, Elizabeth looked back, from a distance, and fancied that over the sacred dust of her beloved dead, there still lingered the glory of her transfiguration. Nearing home, she was met by Jacob, wandering uncertainly in the waning light, in search of her.

"Jacob," she confided, as they retraced their

steps together, "I have had a vision of Heaven. Our Lord has granted me a glimpse into the future life—and all is well."

With Jacob's arm about her, they paused for a moment under the brooding branches of their great memorial oak. Then, crossing the threshold, they seated themselves in their old armchairs, and Elizabeth related her dream.

The heart of Jacob, too, was kindled, and his face was alight with an inner glow. Reverently he opened the well-worn Book that had guided their steps throughout their long life's journey.

The path of the just is as the shining light, he read, *that shineth more and more unto the perfect day.*

A silence fell upon them. Then softly, at evening's close, the voices of Elizabeth and Jacob joined in their vesper hymn:

"Come, let us anew our journey pursue,
    Roll round with the year,
And never stand still till the Master appear.
His adorable will let us gladly fulfill,
    And our talents improve,
By the patience of hope and the labor of love.

Our life is a dream; our time, as a stream,
    Glides swiftly away,

191

And the fugitive moment refuses to stay.
The arrow is flown, the moment is gone;
   The millennial year
Rushes on to our view, and eternity's here.

O that each in the day of his coming may say,
   'I have fought my way through;
I have finished the work thou didst give me
     to do!'
O that each from his Lord may receive the glad
     word,
   'Well and faithfully done!
Enter into my joy, and sit down on my throne!' "

AMEN.

1. Come, let us a-new our jour-ney pur-sue, Roll round with the year,

And nev-er stand still till the Mas-ter ap-pear. His a-dor-a-ble will let us

glad-ly ful-fill, And our tal-ents im-prove, By the pa-tience of hope, and the

la-bor of love, By the pa-tience of hope, and the la-bor of love. A-MEN.

CPSIA information can be obtained at www.ICGtesting.com
Printed in the USA
LVOW090049171112

307573LV00002B/122/A